Praise for *The Magic of Special Children*

"*The Magic of Special Children* is much more than a book about special needs children. It is a love song to Astrid Cheney's extraordinary daughter, Dorica, who has much to teach readers It is also a memoir about Astrid's own childhood in war-torr Germany and her extraordinary family. From them she inherited the resilience, joy, and intuitive sense that would serve her well later in life, as Dorica's mother.

This book draws on Astrid's twenty-five years of experience as an educator and special needs advocate to provide, in Part Three, a remarkable guide for caretakers, teachers, and parents. Here she discusses everything from choosing schools and transitioning to adult services, to the importance of self-care for the caretaker, such as cultivating patience and building a support community. I urge you to open this book and begin to enjoy its many gifts and the wisdom that Astrid Cheney and Dorica have to share with us all."

—Lucy McCauley, editor of the *Travelers' Tales* anthologies (Spain), *A Woman's Path, Women in the Wild,* and *Best Women's Travel Writing (2005-2009)*

"Astrid Cheney draws from her experiences both as mother and professional teacher to offer advice and guidelines to help parents and teachers better care for special children. She weaves her love and devotion into this intimate narrative about mothering her special needs daughter, Dorica. Without sugar-coating the extreme demands on her patience and energy, Astrid takes us inside Dorica's special world where we discover unconditional love, boundless joy, synergy with nature, and remarkable spirituality."

—Emily Rodavich, author, *Mystical Interludes: An Ordinary Person's Extraordinary Experiences*

"Enter the magical world of Dorica, an amazing Bodhisattva spirit who brings joy to everyone around her. Through the astute observations and open mind of her mother and author of this inspiring book, Astrid Cheney, we can behold the spiritual purpose of 'special needs' children. Personally I feel lucky to have met Dorica and passed muster. I spent an afternoon laughing with her and communing with the trees. Don't miss the opportunity to read this heart-opening book."

—Maura McCarley Torkildson, author, *The Inner Tree: Discovering the Roots of Your Intuition and Overcoming Barriers to Mastering It*

"*The Magic of Special Children* is a gift—to all parents of children who are different, and to all children who experience the world through a different lens. It is a mother's love letter to her daughter—one that opens a window into a world that too many people view with pity and heartbreak. This book shows us what we can't always see even when it's right before us—that children with 'disabilities' have abilities that elude most of us. In this poignant, personal story, Astrid Cheney invites all parents to ask: What gifts does my child give to me?"

—Raymond L. Rigoglioso, author, *Gay Men and The New Way Forward*

The Magic of Special Children

The Remarkable Story of Dorica

With a Guide for Parents and Teachers,
Plus a Resource Appendix

ASTRID CHENEY

Copyright © 2021 by Astrid Cheney. All rights reserved. No part of this book may be used or reproduced in any manner whatsoever without the prior written permission except in the case of brief quotations included in critical articles and reviews. For information, address Permissions@ CitrinePublishing.com. The views expressed in this work are solely those of the author and foreword author and do not necessarily reflect the views of the the publisher.

Limit of Liability/Disclaimer of Warranty: While the publisher and authors have used their best efforts in preparing this book, they make no representations or warranties with respect to the accuracy or completeness of the contents of this book and specifically disclaim any implied warranties of merchantability or fitness for a particular purpose. The authors of this book do not dispense medical advice or prescribe the use of any technique as a form of treatment for physical, emotional, or medical problems without the advice of a physician. The intent of the authors is only to offer information of a general nature to help you in your quest for well-being. In the event you use any of the information in the book for yourself, which is your constitutional right, the authors and publisher assume no responsibility for your actions. This is a work of nonfiction. Nonetheless, some names, identifying details, and personal characteristics of the individuals involved have been changed.

Cover Art and Illustrations by Chantal Wolf

Library of Congress Cataloging-in-Publication Data

Cheney, Astrid
The Magic of Special Children: The Remarkable Story of Dorica with a Guide for Parents and Teachers, Plus a Resource Appendix

p. cm.
Paperback ISBN: 978-1-947708-64-8 • Ebook ISBN: 978-1-947708-69-3
Library of Congress Control Number: 2021910266
First Edition, July 2021

CITRINE PUBLISHING
Brasstown, North Carolina, U.S.A.
(828) 585-7030
Publisher@CitrinePublishing.com

DEDICATION

I dedicate this book to Dorica, who inspired me with her unconditional love to finally write this book for all her seen and unseen Special Needs universal friends.

I am grateful for Brian and Howard for having supported and cared for Dorica and me on our journey together.

And thank you, Terra, for stepping in and becoming Dorica's passionate sister, buddy, and best friend.

CONTENTS

Dedication		v
Acknowledgements		ix
Foreword		xiii
Introduction		xv
Chapter 1	A Mother's Journey from East to West	1
Chapter 2	Growing Up with Dorica	15
Chapter 3	Dorica's Unusual Gifts	33
Chapter 4	Who *Is* Dorica?	53
Chapter 5	Practical Suggestions for Parents with Special Needs Children	63
Chapter 6	Practical Suggestions for Teachers and Other Educators Who Serve Special Needs Children	91
Chapter 7	Into the Future	107
Appendix	Tools and Resources for Parents, Caregivers, and Teachers	115
About the Author		123
About the Illustrator		124
Publisher's Note		125

ACKNOWLEDGEMENTS

*T*his book would not have been written without the encouragement and support of my dedicated mentor, Marguerite Rigoglioso, Ph.D. She was the one who first suggested that the story of my daughter, Dorica, and I would inspire other parents of special needs children. A scholar/practitioner of the ancient Mediterranean mystery traditions, Marguerite mentors women and men as a spiritual teacher and clairvoyant guide, helping others cultivate their spiritual knowledge and sacred calling. That is certainly what she did for me a few years ago when I enrolled in one of her classes, "The Divine Birth Mysteries."

As a class assignment, we were asked to work on a ministry project we cared deeply about. What better way to talk about my work with Dorica, who I felt had extraordinary abilities. Marguerite immediately picked up on my intuition, and with her coaching we started on a manuscript. Over the months that followed, this book became alive and started breathing on its own. A birth of a different kind had taken place. It was such a joy to work with Marguerite, and I am deeply thankful to her and the inspiration she provided in our work together, which is still ongoing.

I also want to thank Raymond Rigoglioso, Marguerite's brother and author of the soulful *Gay Men and the New Way Forward*. Ray took over the editing phase of my final manuscript. This was not an easy task since English is not my first language. But like Marguerite, he was patient and caring, guiding me through chapter after chapter.

I would like to acknowledge Lucy McCauley for her very helpful editing on this book.

Especially grateful I am to Citrine Publishing for working on the final touches for the publication of this work with Penelope Love, Chantal Wolf (illustrations), Emily Rodavich (proofreading), and Todd Monahan.

I want to thank Ruth-Inge Heinze, Ph.D., Asian Studies at UC Berkeley, who invited me to the annual International Shaman's Conference to learn about Alternative Modes of Healing. Through her I learned about the Grandmother Winifred Foundation that encourages women over fifty-four to work on projects in the educational or spiritual fields. The foundation's grant allowed me to buy my first computer and start a tutoring center in Oakland, California for students and their parents who needed help in math and other homework. That old computer also wrote this book.

I wish to thank my spiritual teachers, especially Guru Mark Griffin, from Los Angeles, who founded the Hard Light Center of Awakening. He taught me how very remarkable our special needs children are, and he brought me to India to the site where Meher Baba worked with the Special Ones. There I felt firsthand the deep love and devotion that infused that place, and I will always feel endlessly grateful for that exposure.

Also I want to thank Terra Cheney, Dorica's half-sister, for her unwavering love for Dorica and her help in writing this book. Many inspirational ideas came from her. She will be the one who will support this book too and bring it into the future.

I want to thank Patricia Cookinham, who was the first one who looked at the ideas in the manuscript and gave it a full "yes" to move forward. I am also deeply indebted to all my teachers, professors, mothers, fathers, guides, and groups who have taught me on so many levels over the years. Deepest thanks as well to my two supportive husbands, who were so instrumental in enabling me to care for Dorica. Their soft shoulders to lean on helped me on so many levels. I cannot ever say Thank You enough.

I want to give thanks to my parents for encouraging me to find the bridge from science to compassion and a way to be comfortable in either world. They taught me that life is truly a journey worth taking.

Lastly, I want to thank all the Special Ones I've had a chance to meet over the years, who opened my eyes to the possibilities of living in peace and harmony and caring on a much deeper level. And thank you, Dorica, for choosing me to be your mother.

FOREWORD

When I first met Astrid Cheney's daughter, Dorica, it was just as Astrid writes in the pages that follow: I felt as though she were penetrating through to my core, assessing the very quality of my soul. As the gaze of this unusual forty-something girl/woman continued to meet mine for suspended moments, I wondered, almost nervously, if I would pass the test.

And then, slowly, the smile spread over her face. I knew I had been accepted—and not just by a person who now considered me a friend. It was as though I had been accepted unconditionally by some kind of divine intelligence. It was only then that I came into a fuller understanding of who this woman Dorica was. Having heard various stories about her in my work as a teacher and mentor with Astrid over the years, I had gleaned as much, but now I knew Dorica was truly a special being.

With this realization, I also instantly recognized that so many—perhaps most—of the children we label "special needs" at best, or "retarded," "disabled," "handicapped," or "deformed" at worst, are similarly gifted.

It was then that I really began to encourage Astrid to write this book. Because I knew that, in doing so, we would be helping many to awaken to a much broader sense of the diversity of the human family and the gifts that so many special ones bring.

The Magic of Special Children is a fascinating look into what can happen when we embrace special children as possessing, if we see them with the right consciousness, exalted qualities. It is a lesson in how treating them with a positive attitude, unconditional love, and imagination and ingenuity can help bring out their particular qualities, qualities that can truly bless not only their own lives, but also the lives of all those they come in contact with—and perhaps even beyond. Astrid's experience raising Dorica is a lesson in understanding that special children, and the adults they grow up to be, are not only our teachers; they can actually be gurus in the spiritual sense, once their magical qualities are appreciated. Astrid offers a living example and plentiful practical advice for how to bring out the gifts of those children now incarnating who are outside the expected parameters in terms of their genetics, bodily forms, or cognitive functioning.

This book is not only a guide for how we might treat special children and adults better. It also invites deep and fascinating questions about who these human beings may really be, where they may have come from, and what they may be here to do.

In the end, in giving us a glimpse into Dorica, the phenomenon of special children, and her own remarkable spiritual journey, Astrid Cheney points us to a road that goes ever deeper into the Mystery.

I feel blessed to know Astrid and Dorica, and I suspect that in reading about their story and in receiving Astrid's well-earned wisdom about how to raise and work with a magical child, you will, too.

Marguerite Rigoglioso, Ph.D.
Founding Director, Seven Sisters Mystery School,
and author, *The Mystery Tradition of Miraculous Conception: Mary and the Lineage of Virgin Births*

INTRODUCTION

In a world that values accomplishment and success over all else, what contributions do children with different abilities make? What roles can and do they play in society?

All parents of special needs children face these fundamental questions. I believe that, to truly answer them, we must look beyond traditional measures of a child's capacity. We must question our assumptions about what it means to contribute to society. If we open our hearts, minds, and eyes, we will recognize the incredible gifts that special needs children and adults offer us.

Others have written about this topic but few have explored the extraordinary spiritual capabilities that these children bring to us.

This is what this book is all about.

In addition, it provides, not usually found in these stories, a wealth of practical guidance and resources for parents, educators, and caretakers of these remarkable individuals.

The Magic of Special Children begged to be written almost the minute my daughter, Dorica, was born more than fifty years ago. It chronicles my journey raising a special needs child and seeing her through to adulthood. As the years progressed, more and more I began to call myself most fortunate to have been chosen by her to be her mother. Through triumphs and hardships, I have been Dorica's supporter and caregiver—her guiding star. And yet, the reverse holds true as well. Dorica has been my guiding star—my teacher and beacon of light. That is part of the magic of special children—they lead us as much as we guide them.

The book has three major parts. In Part One, I write from my own experience as a child in wartime Germany through young adulthood, and about the people around me. My grandmother, especially, influenced me profoundly and encouraged my skills and intuition that would later prove so important for raising Dorica. Part Two chronicles Dorica's growth and development from babyhood to adulthood and how she manifested her unique gifts.

The last part of the book, Part Three, offers a practical guide for parents, teachers, caretakers, and educators. Here I write both as a mother and an educator who taught Elementary School in the Oakland School District for twenty-five years. In these chapters I include my discoveries and experience with Dorica and other children to focus on questions that might help other parents. What is it about special needs children that makes caring for them so worthwhile and rewarding? How do we take care of them and somehow stay positive and in-tune with who they are? How do we do all of that while also holding a job, nurturing ourselves, and/or keeping a marriage or other relationships alive?

The final chapter addresses some of the newest thinking and discoveries about our special children, and takes a look at what the future could hold. Speaking from my own experience at home and as a teacher, I offer practical suggestions that might help caretakers facing long-term care arrangements and challenging changes in the years to come.

At the end of the book you will find a Question and Answer section for discussion groups or book clubs, designed to develop more understanding around the lives of the Special Ones who are all around us but seldom really noticed or acknowledged. There I include my website information and an invitation to hear from you—I look forward to sharing experiences, ideas, and resources.

Are you ready? Let's get started.

The Magic of Special Children

The Remarkable Story of Dorica

Chapter 1

A MOTHER'S JOURNEY FROM EAST TO WEST

My grandmother loved to tell the story of how I, as a one-year-old baby, saved our whole family. It was at the end of World War II that the Russians would often enter German people's homes, steal what they wanted, and even kill parents in front of their children. One day, troops entered and attempted to plunder our home. I must have noticed one soldier in particular. I reached out my arms to him. My grandmother let me go since I was smiling at him. She let him hold me. He embraced me and I gave him a kiss. That stopped the whole group of soldiers in their tracks. They all left.

This story was often repeated throughout my childhood. I realize now that the experience encapsulated my entire approach to life, something I was blessed to be born with, which is responding to challenging circumstances with love. Throughout my life I've seen how love can turn a potential tragedy into a blessing. That is what happened when I gave birth to Dorica.

My daughter, Dorica, was born with mental retardation, or intellectual difference, as we would call it today. We don't really know why she has this condition. It's possible that she was deprived of oxygen during my long labor with her, but we can't be certain. As of this writing, Dorica is fifty-one years old, yet she still operates on the level of a two-year-old—a child in an adult body. She has a limited vocabulary and ability to learn, and she walks with difficulty. And yet, as I have mothered and protected her over the years, I have come to realize just how special she is. I have often questioned who is nurturing whom.

Since she was born, I have always felt that Dorica entered my life for a reason. She makes me happy, has given me a purpose, and has expanded my consciousness. We have always been close. We have furthered each other's development. We have a deep and profound understanding of each other. We are two individual souls, yet it often feels that we are one.

But to tell Dorica's story I need to begin with my own.

Growing up in Eastern Germany

I was born in November 1944 in Eastern Germany, at the end of World War II. This was a very trying time for my family. Shortly after my mother became pregnant with me, my father was captured by the Russians and sent to a labor camp in Siberia. My mother moved in with my grandparents and managed to survive through incredible difficulties. Through it all, my mother never doubted that her husband was still alive. She always knew that he would show up one day.

During that time, we lived in a little village on the outskirts of Berlin. Woods surrounded our small house with a garden, and made the setting peaceful, magical, and comforting. Our family was isolated in many ways, but we had neighbors within walking distance. Other towns were a few miles away, farms even further. Potsdam, the "major" city, had just one store, a post office, a train station, a bus stop, a school, and one doctor. It was reachable by a half-hour bus ride.

My grandparents had settled in the village before the Russian occupation. My grandfather was a banker before the war and continued working there. My grandmother was the artist in the family, painting portraits for townspeople. My mother worked in town as a secretary until I was born.

The Russian occupation, which began in 1945, took a toll on this idyllic setting. The Russians would move into abandoned buildings, destroy what was left, and find ways to punish the German people. One way they did this was to severely restrict the number of daily calories people could eat, which they enforced through a system of cards that got stamped at the grocery store. Butter and oil were nowhere to be found. Everyone went hungry, even the wealthy.

When I was a baby, my mother found milk on the black market. She would hide it on her body—a most difficult task—because she knew she had to pass Russian checkpoints. If the Russians found the milk, they would dump it.

Eventually, my mother found a dependable farmer miles away who would leave a small bucket of milk and some butter hidden just outside his gate. To remain undetected by the Russians and their dogs, my mother would leave me with my grandparents and travel at night to the farm, whether it was raining or not, through the deep forest and streams. In the last years of her life she told me that she felt my protecting presence around her on these nightly trips through the woods. I became her guiding star.

I can only imagine what it must have been like for her. My mom developed an inner strength that kept me alive even under these most arduous of circumstances. I believe I instinctively learned two important lessons from her through these trials: First, no matter how hard life can be, people can show mercy and compassion to help us get through. Second, once we are called upon to complete a task, we can't give up—no matter how long it takes.

Throughout these first years of my life, my mom landed many outside jobs, typing dissertations and papers for professors and professionals. I never went hungry and was always cared for. Everyone in my little family did their part. We were not rich—we merely survived.

My Early Years and My Father's Return

Just as my mother had always predicted, my father returned home when I was five years old, years after the war had ended. He had managed to escape from the Siberian Russian labor camp, traveling four months on foot. He walked mostly at night and received help from many people who could have easily turned him in.

Before his capture, he and my mother had chosen baby names for a boy and a girl. My father instinctively knew he had a girl. My name Astrid, which he had chosen for me, held great meaning for him. He wanted to have a star daughter that could communicate and travel with him long distances. My mother seemed to totally agree with him. Therefore, he named me Astrid, originating from the word 'astro' or 'astra', meaning "star." Just as my mother experienced throughout her long journeys at night, my father felt my presence with him. He knew he needed to make it back. I had been his guiding star too.

My dad loved me from the minute he laid eyes on me. I accepted him wholeheartedly too. I felt I had gained a real playmate. He would play horse with me and let me ride on his shoulders on longer walks. He taught me how to play ball against the house and flew kites with me.

He was very serious, but he also had a sense of humor. I felt safe and protected by him. When I began school, my dad shared his interest in math and science with me. He took me to observatories where we would spend hours watching the night sky through telescopes. He told me about the myths of the star constellations, which I loved hearing. My dad's influence inspired me to become seriously interested in space exploration: I wanted to be one of the people who traveled to Mars.

My father was a mathematician, and he was able to secure employment as a cartographer for the East German government in Berlin. This gave our family financial stability for the first time in my childhood.

As soon as I understood the basics of math, he gave me puzzles to solve. For instance: Why can't we divide by zero? The answer: It becomes infinity. He would ask, "Why does our counting system start with zero?" The Egyptians and Greek philosophers, he told me, had lengthy debates on the topic. By introducing me to math and science, my father laid the foundation for my own quest for knowledge.

When I was six years old, my brother was born. We were all still living with my grandparents at the time. Because of the age difference between my brother and me, I took on the roles of teacher, playmate, caretaker, and big sister. We had fun together and developed a bond that has lasted for a lifetime. Today he is still my "little brother," despite the fact that he is much, much taller.

My father's two-hour commute to Berlin eventually grew tiresome, so a year later my parents bought a home in East Berlin. They had to decide where I should live. My grandmother wanted me to stay with her, as she and I had grown very close. I loved this idea because she was so gentle and loving. My mother and father moved with my brother to East Berlin, and I remained with my grandmother. At the beginning it was hard not seeing my family that often, especially my brother I missed a lot, but I had a chance to become more independent and resilient. I knew they loved me and that mattered the most.

My grandparents raised me for the next three years. During this time, my grandmother—the magician in the family—became a major influence on me. She was caring and compassionate. She loved the woods and the outdoors and had many friends. She was beautiful, a true artist, and insightful. It was always a joy to be around her.

I eagerly listened as she imparted her knowledge about spirits, mushrooms, healing plants, and how to prepare potions. She taught me the way of the shaman and what it means to care for people and the Earth. Her positivity rubbed off on me. My grandmother died when I was eleven years old, but I always felt her spirit around me. I still do to this day.

When my grandmother passed away I had to move to my parents' place in East Berlin. However, we spent every two weekends in my grandmother's house and cared for my grandfather who was still alive, which was a real blessing since I could still use this time to roam around in nature.

Escape to West Germany

When I was thirteen, my parents decided to flee East Germany and escape to the West. They believed in freedom and choice, which ran contrary to the philosophy of the Eastern Bloc. My mother and father did not tell my brother and me about the plan until the day before we left. They feared we might talk about it and thus endanger our safety and chances to escape. They gave us one day to say goodbye to everyone and everything we knew.

I wasn't really surprised, however. People were fleeing to the West in great numbers at that time, almost 10,000 a day in 1957. The prospect of living in the West excited me. I looked forward to what it could offer, and to our new life there. But first, I would have to say goodbye to my friends. I knew I would never see or even write them again. We would become refugees.

My parents chose Easter and school vacation time for our escape. My mother organized the whole plan. She gave our maid and cook two weeks off. My girlfriend would care for my canary. Grandfather would come with us. The holiday would give us a good reason to travel from Potsdam to our home in East Berlin. None of our neighbors would suspect anything out of the ordinary—we would just be leaving for Easter vacation.

My mother explained to me that we would live with relatives in Nuremberg, in West Germany. We would have to pass through many Russian security checkpoints to get to the West. She taught us what to say to the officials and how to answer their questions. She drilled into our brains the phone number of our relatives, but she did not tell us the address where we would stay, so we could not divulge it to the police if questioned.

My mother asked me to carefully choose a keepsake that I could bring with me that would fit into my side pocket. She instructed me to say nothing about our plans to my friends, as their knowledge of our whereabouts would jeopardize our safety and theirs if the police questioned them.

The next day—my last day—I went purposefully to all my close girlfriends' houses and played silly games with them. I wanted to make them laugh for the very last time with me, like we always did every time we got together. I did not tell them what my family was about to do.

I rode my bike across town and luckily found my boyfriend chopping wood outside his house. I wished him Happy Easter. He seemed very pleased that I came by. We joked, laughed, and kidded around like always. I knew he would later realize this was my "goodbye" gesture. He had earned that respect. But of course, I did not tell him that we were leaving.

I walked through the woods one more time and asked the spirits to keep us safe. I went to my grandmother's graveyard and talked to her. I was ready. I was glad my mom was already in East Berlin since I had so many things to do. She might have become sentimental, while I had begun to look forward to this adventure.

That evening I cleaned my room. I thought about what people might find and what I would let them find. My collection of sweet love letters with poems from my boyfriend had to go—the police might question him. I redistributed my books throughout the house so as to leave no trace of my real interests. My mother had already taken with her the money I had saved. Pictures that accompanied the letters also needed to be discarded.

I went through my treasures one by one and said my goodbyes. I could not find my favorite doll, which I thought might be just as well. Little did I know my mother already had collected it and other special things of mine that I could not carry. I had a stove in my room, in which I burned everything: pictures, letters, stamp collections, favorite clothes, card games, toys, and more. When I was done purging those things I felt absolutely great. It was as if I'd somehow needed to extract my soul from these material things so I could leave a clean, fresh place for the people who would move in. I wanted to wish them well and welcome them.

Grandfather did similarly—he was up way into the night. It was just he and I in the house, and we left each other alone. He coughed a lot, though. He had already seen a doctor when my mom was there. We knew he had developed pneumonia, but going to a hospital was out of the question since we had to leave in the morning. I worried about my grandfather all night and whether he would make it. Somehow he summoned a mysterious strength over night. Grandfather and I left the next morning. I snuck some cough drops for him into my pocket.

I slid something else into my pocket—a broken small red coral bead necklace, a gift from my grandmother years earlier. It had no monetary value, but it had a whole story behind it. She had given it to me on one of my earlier birthdays as a gift from my great-grandmother before she passed away. I was not supposed to wear it to school, since it was too delicate. Well, I tried to show off to my girlfriends and wore it to school. The string broke and all the pieces fell on the floor. I collected as much as I could, but I was really embarrassed.

I went home and mustered up the courage and told my grandmother the truth. She told me that I needed to get back to the dump pile in school and sift through the garbage to find some more beads. It sure was a lesson for me. She did not shout or scold me. Just going back to the dump was enough punishment. I did go back to the school dump and spent quite some time looking for the beads. I found two more. I felt like heaven had mercy on me even in this predicament. Grandmother did not say one more word and I knew she would not fix this heirloom necklace. These leftover beads I took with me on my journey. I knew they would protect me.

When Grandfather and I left the next morning, neither of us looked back. He taught me how to navigate the journey and not raise suspicions. We would take a bus to a train. The police would search our passports, give us body pat-downs, and question us.

My father and brother waited for our train at another station and got on. We did not greet each other. We needed to stay separate. We got off at a station in West Berlin and walked to one of my mother's friend's house. We took different streets but finally all met there. Our family was back together, but we were not safe yet. We took taxis at different times to the airport.

My mother's friend had arranged our plane tickets under misspelled names since the Russians periodically checked names. The flight to Nuremberg lasted two hours. After we made it through the controls and security checkpoints, our relatives from my father's side picked us up. We had entered the Western territory. Now we were refugees like thousands before us. Each day thousands of East Germans left their homes and escaped by various ways to the West.

Three weeks later, the famous Berlin Wall was built and completed in a few days. Very few escaped afterwards. We were lucky. We took almost the last flight out of the East.

My dad's relatives let us stay with them so we would not have to enter the refugee camps. The five of us settled into a small room with a shared bath in one of their garden houses.

As soon as we arrived, my mother tried to admit my grandfather to a hospital. Because we did not have refugee status yet, nor any identification with our new address, we would have had to register with agencies for services, which would have taken too long. Given his condition, he needed care right away. My mom arranged to see a private doctor. It cost an inordinate amount of money, but it worked. He got better and pulled through. He had also taken medicine from his old doctor in East Germany, and I made sure he ate all of the cough drops I had in my pocket.

As refugees in the West, our circumstances had once again changed dramatically. We went from living in a spacious home with a cook and maid to five of us sharing one room. We had to ask for every spoon and bar of soap. The year we spent there was not easy, but we adjusted. At the time I wondered, *why on Earth did we leave?* Looking back I appreciate and am grateful for my parents' choice. They cherished freedom above anything—freedom to move, to talk freely, to become educated. It was priceless. They gave us the precious gift of freedom.

It was a very difficult time for everyone, but we survived as a family. My mother found a job as a secretary after a few months. My highly skilled father needed more time to find work, almost a year. My grandfather received a small government retirement pension, which we all lived on for a while.

School and friends were also a challenge. My new classmates had already learned English and French, which put me three years behind. My good Russian language skills, necessary to survive in East Germany, did not help me. My new girlfriends would buy lipstick and face lotion, which I could not afford. They were silly and goofy while I was serious and sensitive. They saw me as an uneducated Eastern girl and sometimes made me feel inferior.

Still, I always knew that the challenges I faced would be temporary. Seeing how my parents struggled and sacrificed, I felt it was important to remain positive for our family. If freedom was our goal, then sticking it out gave me the best chance to achieve it. In my earlier years, I had read Karl May's books, which were popular among preteens in Germany. His books vividly described America and the desert. Those images captured my imagination and became a beacon and a goal for me—I would make it through, and I would travel to see those places myself.

I became a guiding light for my family. I took it upon myself to support our common mission to succeed in the West, and they came to depend on me. I felt like a shaman as I began to communicate with my guides and spirits in all the ways my grandmother had taught me. I knew they would help me get through. Slowly my inner strength and power returned. I let go of the past and embraced our new journey together.

Things began to look up when my father landed employment in cartography. We moved to Munich and found an apartment that had enough space for us. My father's income enabled me to get an allowance for the first time. My mother surprised me with the money that I had saved in the East and that she had needed to use for our escape. She had not forgotten about it. That was an old family tradition that we always returned what we had borrowed, even within our family. It can be years, but it will be returned. She showed me by example and I appreciated this.

I found a nice circle of girlfriends and began taking ballroom dancing lessons. My brother joined the school band and made friends too. We both felt happier. In summertime we even were able to go on vacations to the Mediterranean tourist spots.

Around this time, Grandfather had a stroke. We cared for him at home until it was his time to leave the planet. I was the last person he spoke to. This taught me an important lesson: Leave no one behind. We brought Grandfather with us wherever we moved. He gave me the gift of truly understanding me, and I understood him.

He loved cigars and I remember that on Sundays he would smoke them and even once in a while light up his pipe. It was like medicine for him, and I enjoyed the aroma around the house. It was also a meditation for him, blowing smoke circles into the air and enjoying life and maybe even communicating with his spirit guides. He loved nature and could and would mix birch sap and herbs for his special hair concoction. True enough, he had full hair until the day he died.

My Husband Brian and The Birth of Dorica

I met Brian in my school in Munich when I was eighteen years old. An American, Brian had come with his family to live in Germany while his father attended the University. My teacher assigned Brian to me, to help him learn German. He was funny, very smart, and interesting. I told Brian about my dream of becoming a shaman and seeing the American desert, and he told me stories about the Native Americans. This kind of inspiration was exactly what I needed. Brian and I liked each other and were well matched from the beginning.

I liked Brian's family a lot too. Brian's dad had made a documentary for National Geographic about the Mexican rainforest and the pyramids. His family had traveled around the world, which spoke to my own dreams of traveling in the future. Their time in Germany would not last long, however. Brian's father would soon complete his studies in Psychology after two years and was eager to return to the United States with his family.

Brian learned German very quickly and could translate for his father. It impressed me to no end.

Brian promised that he would return to Germany as soon as he turned twenty-one. We wrote love letters back and forth by mail. He would have to cross an ocean to be with me, however, so I couldn't be certain he would return. I dated and had some boyfriends. Brian always maintained his intention to follow through on his promise, which gave me reason to keep a little hope alive. A year later, he was on a flight back to Munich.

Immediately, Brian started looking for a job. He landed work doing translations, and he became a clerk at an electronics store. He found a little room for rent (which did not allow girlfriends). I started working at the Max-Planck Institute as a secretary and bookkeeper for several professors. I planned to attend university and become either a doctor or a biochemist, but first I needed to earn money for such an adventure. Brian and I were determined to survive without any help from either of our parents. At that time, I still lived at home.

Two years later we had both saved enough money for our first apartment, but I would not move in with him until we were married. He proposed to me when I was twenty-three years old. We got married in a church wedding in Germany.

Brian made all of us laugh by his insistence on an American custom – kissing at the altar - in the wedding ceremony. The Protestant church I belonged to, and in which we would be married, required Brian to attend marriage classes so he could learn the church's history and traditions. Brian's parents were Protestants too but were not devoted church-goers.

Brian upset the pastor because he wanted to kiss me after we were pronounced husband and wife. This was a "no-no" in Germany. No kissing was allowed in church, period. Of course, Brian was determined to do so and I could see what it meant to him. I loved it.

Brian's insistence to kiss me in church became the topic of conversation during our classes and among my family. Finally, the pastor gave in. He agreed he would look the other way and "not see" the kiss, nor would he announce it. Talk about bending the rules! Brian's dad, who attended the wedding, found the whole debacle to be quite humorous.

We had a beautiful ceremony in the church. Brian kept his word and kissed me in front of everyone. We moved into our first apartment in Munich. Brian was always loving and caring, no matter what the circumstances.

Before we could really relax and enjoy our life together, I became pregnant with Dorica. We had been building a foundation for our life together and working hard, and suddenly we were about to become parents. We hardly had time to breathe.

And yet we eagerly anticipated the arrival of our new child. We had fun imagining what this creation would look like and how smart this child would be. Brian wanted a girl and I wanted a boy. We talked about our future. Brian wanted to settle down and build a loudspeaker business; I wanted to travel the world with Brian (and maybe with baby). We had fun with it. We instinctively knew it would work out.

I remember the magical day we conceived Dorica. It was around Christmastime, when the city of Munich is decked out like a fairyland, and one can hear music everywhere. Brian and I went to an organ concert at the Frauenkirche, a church in Munich. The organ concerts at that time of the year are exquisitely beautiful. Brian, who played the piano, especially loved piano and organ music.

Attending the concert was almost like renewing our vows, since our first date was at a church organ concert in a small town. It was magical then and I knew it would be magic again. Brian and I would hold hands and enjoy the vibration of the music.

And magic it was. The organ touched my heart. It lifted me up, and I totally forgot where I was. Brian moved and swayed his body to the celestial music. We loved the music, we loved each other, and we felt ecstatic together. Music transported us into higher realms.

We went home. It was cold outside, but our apartment was warm and cozy. It was the perfect night to snuggle up. I felt like a goddess in Brian's arms. This night was different—it was a holy night. In my mind, Brian was a Greek god who was seducing me, the virgin goddess. I instinctively felt that we both entered a higher realm to create a special being.

Waves and waves of electricity washed over us, flashing waves, blessed by the church of the Holy Maria that we visited earlier with the music still in our bones. It was magic and ecstasy in the purest form. We felt blessed. We both felt it. The world around us disappeared.

Dorica was born September 19, 1968, in Munich, Germany. She entered this world as a special being as I will describe in the chapters that follow.

Chapter 2

GROWING UP WITH DORICA

*"I have only love to give,
and all I want is love."*
—Meher Baba, *The Silent Master*,
Meher Baba Archives

The news of my pregnancy brought me tremendous joy. I knew we had conceived that night, and I could not wait to welcome our baby into the world. The pregnancy itself proceeded quite ordinarily as far as I can remember. Routine visits to the doctors all indicated that the baby was healthy and growing normally. What could possibly go wrong? Brian and I began to seriously plan for the future with our new child.

I knew Brian would make an excellent father. He was warm, positive, compassionate, imaginative, and full of life. He was the sweetest, most loving, and most romantic man I had ever met. Our love for each other gave us a strong foundation for parenthood.

Despite an easy pregnancy, labor with Dorica took a long time— thirty-two hours. After spending the night at the hospital in childbirth, I received some medication to speed up the process. Dorica might have suffered from oxygen loss, but no one could say for certain. Apart from that, I had no other complications. Somehow I knew Dorica would be just fine. When Dorica finally showed up I could not help saying, *"Das hast du gut gemacht"* ("You did great"). In retrospect, this little phrase set the stage for a lifetime of teamwork betweeen Dorica and me.

Still, it took me a few days to adjust to the reality of having a girl. I had wanted a boy. Throughout my pregnancy, I imagined the adventures he and I would have—hiking in the jungle, climbing trees, even traveling to the moon. I thought that a girl would be obsessed with fashion—something I knew or cared little about. Brian, on the other hand, was elated. He imagined her as a little princess and knew they would mutually adore each other.

I wanted to name her Doris, after a beloved doll of mine from childhood. I never tired of changing Doris's clothes or preparing her food. When I played with her, I would imagine the day when I would clothe and feed my own child.

Even when I grew older, I gave Doris a special place in my room. She sat on a small altar surrounded by her clothes. I would regularly put out food for her like nuts and oranges, and I would frame the display with fresh flowers. My parents would laugh at me—they thought it was ridiculous. Many years later, when I moved to the United States I learned about altars and how to keep deities alive and happy by feeding and honoring them. My grandmother had taught me about the ways of shamans and the beings that lived in the woods. It was as if this early initiation gave me intuitive training into the world of spirits and deities.

Brian wanted to name her after his brother Eric. We chose Erica, which is also an evergreen flower that blooms in the fall (spelled "Erika" in German). Finally, her name morphed into Dorica, a perfect combination of masculine and feminine energies, and a meaningful blend for both Brian and me.

Everyone who met Dorica fell in love with her. We certainly did. As I expected, Brian became the sweetest father to her. The first six months passed without much sign of the challenges she would eventually present. I believe Dorica let us enjoy this carefree time so we could create a strong foundation for a lifelong connection.

Dorica and I bonded very early on. She only drank my breast milk and would refuse and spit out formula. Apart from that, she hardly ever cried, and she seemed happy and healthy. Upon examination, our doctor gave her a clean bill of health.

We didn't think much about it when Dorica missed a health marker at three months of age—when she should have been able to sit up on her own. We suspected she might just be a little slow in physical development.

After maternity leave I returned to my job, where I worked as a secretary and bookkeeper. I wanted to stay at home and care for Dorica, but if I did we would lose government benefits that covered pre- and post-natal care and childbirth expenses. I would need to work full-time for a year to not lose those benefits. I promised Dorica that I would care for her at home after a year and make up for lost time.

We left Dorica in a state-run nursery during the day. Brian took a full-time job as a translator. All throughout that time, I began to worry: Why would Dorica not sit up? Did something go wrong? Did we fail her? Did we not give her enough love or attention? Brian tried to cheer me up when I started worrying, and I cheered him up when he started worrying.

When the one-year point passed I left my job. We all felt relieved, and Dorica sensed this positive change. After the first week at home with her, she gave us a special gift: She sat up on her own. I cannot describe how elated it made us. Any parent whose child has finally accomplished something after many attempts understands the experience. It was like a miracle. It gave us hope.

Our joy was short-lived, however. Despite the fact that she could now sit up, she could not crawl—let alone walk—and she did not make sounds or babble like other babies her age. She seemed perfectly content to visit parks with us and enjoy nature. She would become completely still and listen to the birds singing to each other, as if she understood their language but not ours. By the time she turned one and a half, we realized we needed to seek expert advice.

We visited several doctors and learned that physical therapy could speed up her muscle development. We took Dorica to a wonderful therapist for hour-long treatments three to four times a week. Dorica loved the sessions and made great progress. After six months of therapy, Dorica began crawling. After eight months, she began to stand and took her first steps. We celebrated these milestones like shipwrecked sailors who had found a life raft. Had we known about physical therapy and its benefits, we would have taken her earlier.

Dorica still wasn't talking—she just made babbling noises. She didn't even say "mama" or "papa." So we went back to the doctors. They performed muscle biopsies, spine tests, hearing tests, vision tests, and more. Every test came back normal.

Finally our physician produced a diagnosis: Dorica had mental retardation (with cerebral palsy but without tremors). While it was an umbrella diagnosis that could include other conditions, at least we knew generally what to expect. He told us that her speech and motor development would remain at the level of a two-year-old. Her progress would get slower, but she might eventually walk. Even today Dorica prefers crawling over walking, and she uses a wheelchair or walker to get around.

Brian and I came to terms with this news in different, but complementary ways. I've never been one to dwell on my feelings, but I wrestled with the question, "Why did this happen to me?" I had dreams, and caring for Dorica full time would interfere with them. I knew I would need to adjust my expectations. So I began looking at the situation from a shamanic perspective: What can I understand about her? Why is she here on Earth? How do other cultures view special needs children?

Brian never got upset or depressed about the news. Being the more emotional of the two of us, he responded by pouring his love into Dorica. We both concluded that we had been called to this task of caring for Dorica. I felt intuitively that she and I had lessons to learn from each other. I still feel this way.

Physical therapy ended for Dorica when she reached the goal of walking on her own. Under our doctor's guidance, when she was two-and-a-half years old we entered her into speech therapy. The approach used music and songs to help her learn how to vocalize. She made very unusual sounds, however. Her vocalizing sounded like Tuva throat singing—a Mongolian art practiced in Mongolia, Tuva, and Siberia. She would throat sing for hours in a very melodic, harmonious way. Dorica became a champion at it.

She began to say a few words, but neither "mama" nor "papa" were among them. I cannot exactly remember her first word, but it was something she wanted, like "mi" for milk. The speech therapist tried sign language and clue cards for objects, but Dorica showed no interest in them. The speech therapist gave up after six months. Dorica could understand around 200 to 300 words but would not verbalize them. This is where the development has its limits, or at least in Dorica's case. She was and has remained on the level of a two-and-a-half year old.

By age three, Dorica could walk, sit, crawl, say a few words, and understand more than a few words. More than anything she was happy and beautiful. We went to playgrounds, parks, and shopping centers, and she crawled on buses and trains. She wanted to see everything and had fun wherever she went. She loved everyone. When people met her, they usually didn't realize that she was slow. When they greeted her, I had to explain to them that she could not talk.

After speech therapy ended, we attended training sessions for parents. We learned what words to teach her, what games to play, and what songs to sing. Now we were on our own.

It began to occur to us that Germany might not be the best place for us to remain given Dorica's special needs. Despite living in Munich, a major city, we could not find a day care center that would take her—because she was not toilet trained. We needed to care for Dorica twenty-four hours per day. That wasn't good for any of us.

By the time Dorica was four she had learned a few more words, but only we could understand them. She still hadn't spoken in sentences. Her demeanor remained the same, however—happy and content. It was a different story with the doctors, though. Dorica began to mistrust them, as they just examined her and made everyone around her nervous and tense. She began playing a role we would come to recognize throughout her life—she provided us guidance about the situation. The doctors were giving us no new information. It was time to move on.

By the time Dorica turned five, we began to explore treatment options in America. Brian's father, a practicing psychologist in Berkeley, California, recommended we visit the area. When we did, we learned about possibilities we could only dream of in Germany. We found special needs care centers, which would provide day care for children with mental retardation, board-and-care homes, nurse practitioners trained in cerebral palsy, and more.

That visit convinced us to relocate. We sold everything and moved to Berkeley, where we stayed with Brian's parents for two months. We found an apartment and enrolled in college. We would work, attend college, and care for Dorica while we searched for the right services for her. We knew we would make it with planning and persistence.

Berkeley

Brian and I made a great team. He developed a workable plan: We would enroll in classes whose times did not overlap. He would work as a translator at night while I tutored students in German at the college in the early morning. Brian started building loudspeakers on the weekends while I taught at the German school on Saturdays in Berkeley. Our schedules were very tight, but we found a way to care for Dorica ourselves until she was six and a half.

By that time, Dorica was still speaking just a few words and had made only minimal developmental progress. Then we found a service that made our great gamble in moving to America pay off: We enrolled her in the Child Special Needs Care Center at Hilltop in Richmond, California. She spent five to six hours there each day, which was a dramatic change from being at home with us all the time. It proved pivotal. She socialized with children her own age and with similar abilities. The wonderful support team provided therapy and stimulating exercises. We knew she was in good hands, and she responded well. We all became much happier. We felt that a load had been lifted off our shoulders.

With Dorica receiving care during the day, I could concentrate on my career. I chose to become a teacher—in large part so my vacations and holidays would coincide with those of Dorica's, and so we could save on babysitting costs. Brian started a business building loudspeakers out of the garage. He too chose his profession because of Dorica—her love of music inspired him to create a world in which she would be surrounded by it.

Brian and I cared for Dorica in our own ways. We did so from our hearts and souls. I believe the reason she hardly ever gave us difficulty was because she felt so accepted and cherished. We rarely raised our voices or got angry at her. We understood it would be useless. In my experience, special needs children want to please their parents. If they act out, it is usually because they are overwhelmed or scared, or they don't know what is happening. They cannot verbalize their worries or hurts, and we must strive to understand what they are trying to convey.

I did lose my temper with Dorica a few times, and it taught me the utter absurdity of yelling at her. One time, for instance, we had visitors coming. I had placed mustard, salt, and pepper on the counter for dinner. When I turned my back, Dorica took these ingredients and mixed them on the counter. I turned around and saw what she had done. Big blobs of yellow mustard dripped from the counter onto the floor. She had poured pepper on top and placed the salt shaker in the mustard. Everything was yellow. The pepper gave me a sneezing fit. She looked at me, proud and happy that she had done that all by herself. I blew up.

Her expression immediately changed—she looked so sorry and seemed to understand that I was upset for some reason. I realized she had no idea why I was angry at her, nor could she comprehend why. It stopped me in my tracks. I apologized to her. Then she ran over to me with open, loving arms. She gave me a kiss and it was over. Done.

That is the magic of Dorica. She gives unconditional love. It is what makes caring for a special child so rewarding.

Brian hardly ever got upset with Dorica. He was gentle and loving to her. She could read him like a book, and she knew what she could get away with. He told me the story of one visit they made to the Albany Bowling Alley, which they frequented together. Everyone knew Brian and Dorica. They kept an eye on her while he played so she could roam freely.

Dorica always seemed to get hungry as soon as they arrived. That night, as Brian played, Dorica went to the snack counter and ordered hot dogs, a coke, fries, milk, and chocolate. It was amazing that she could say those words when she wanted to. They gave her everything she ordered, and at the end of the night Brian had to pay for it all. Dorica would never do that with me, because I would never let her get away with it. When I accompanied them, she would show no interest in food at all.

From my observations, this kind of behavior is typical for special needs children—they adjust based on the people around them. Depending on who they're with, they can express entirely different parts of their personality, and they can even seem like different people.

Even though Dorica attended the special needs care center during the week, Brian and I still had very little time and money for anything fun. We were determined to keep the spark alive between us and remain the loving couple we had always been. We made a firm commitment to have lunch at Denny's once a month. Just the two of us—no Dorica. It was a special treat that we cherished. These kinds of small, loving gestures renewed our connection with each other and reminded us that we were more than just caretakers for Dorica.

Despite our best intentions and utmost care, accidents happened. When she was nine or ten years old, Dorica got burned in the bathtub. Brian was giving Dorica a bath that night when the phone rang. He left for about three minutes. In the meantime Dorica opened the hot water and scalded her back. She has a delayed response to pain, so she did not feel it right away. Finally she started crying and Brian jumped to help.

He rushed her to the hospital, where she spent almost three weeks in the burn unit. Brian blamed himself. It happened so quickly and unexpectedly. Just a few minutes of not watching a handicapped child can wreak havoc in a parent's life, not to mention that of the child. After this incident I developed a habit every night of expressing gratitude for a day that Dorica, Brian, and I made it through without an accident.

While she was in the hospital, Dorica amazed us and everyone else. She had to undergo painful, daily acid baths. She had no language to communicate her needs. She was separated from us, staying in an uncomfortable environment where everything was kept covered to remain sterile. And yet when we showed up, she smiled and gave us no hint of the ordeals she had endured. We only learned about her experiences through the nurses.

We found a way to soothe Dorica's spirit—and ours. We sang old German songs that we used to sing together in Germany. She had not forgotten them, and she joined with us. These songs gave us strength to get through that painful time. Everyone in the burn unit heard and responded to our singing—the doctors, nurses, and patients. No one complained. The nurses told us that two other patients started singing too, and that it helped others who were exhausted from pain to fall asleep. The songs became a cozy blanket for Dorica and everyone in the burn unit. Dorica became the healer. Her singing helped Brian know he could let go of his guilt. Music was their secret language. The songs worked their magic.

When Dorica returned home I worried that she would never take a bath again. But she has always surprised us. She acted like nothing had ever happened and went happily into the bathtub as before. The only thing that changed was that Dorica continued singing the songs we had sung in the hospital. She would sing in the evening, and I loved to join her before she went to sleep. We continued the magic.

When Dorica was ten we enrolled her in an experimental program where she attended a regular school and classroom setting. To our disappointment, she did not like it at all. She sat for hours and could not understand a word anyone said. The regular students ignored her, and the teacher could not spare the extra time Dorica required. Only the aides watched her. Dorica began to regress, wetting her diapers again. She stopped running and walking. Despite the best intentions of the school district, the experiment failed.

When it became clear that Dorica could not function in a school setting, we tried placing her in a work program. Accompanied by an aide, Dorica worked at Popeye's, a fast food chain similar to McDonald's, wiping down tables. She loved the work, and we were thrilled to see her socializing and moving about. Ironically, she would never do this at home. As we had observed in other situations, she expressed an entirely different personality at work.

At a certain point she would get tired of wiping tables and lie down on the floor, making believe she didn't feel well. Customers would come up to her, alarmed, and ask, "Are you okay?" She was fine, of course. She had begun to learn how to "work" people and get their attention or sympathy. She still does today. Unfortunately, this behavior caused disruption in the restaurant, so the management eventually had to let her go.

Aside from this program, which she attended from ages twelve to fourteen, she had no other therapy, outings, or schooling. Due to her inability to perform even the most basic job, the staff at the work program did not offer her another placement.

From ages fourteen to eighteen, Dorica returned to the day care setting at Hilltop. In the time she had been gone, the program had grown to include speech, vocational, music, and physical therapies, and outings into the community. They just had built a new swimming pool, which Dorica adored. She received therapy in the pool to improve her ability to move and walk. She started talking more, using new words, and even making two-word sentences. The staff and aides loved her.

With Dorica at the center during the day, I could complete college. I attended the University of California, Berkeley, where I received my bachelor's and master's degrees. I landed a full-time job teaching fourth grade in Oakland. I loved it and stayed there for the next twenty-five years.

I often wondered how I juggled everything without becoming overstressed. In retrospect, I believe Dorica gave me the strength to get through. The love she poured over me flowed onto my students. The experience I had at home made me more resilient and patient in the classroom. I could sense when my students had fears or problems. They were on a similar level of emotional maturity as Dorica. I applied what I learned from her to them. She became my guide and compass.

Brian continued his business building loudspeakers, which he still ran out of our garage. Dorica would spend hours with him listening to classical music. The two of them would forget to eat or drink. She would sing with the music and even dance to it. They emanated love and joy, always reveling in each other's company and sharing their love of music. Brian's assistants and customers all knew Dorica.

She became the final arbiter of his designs. If she walked out of the garage, that meant, that the sound was not yet perfect. If she stayed, the speakers were ready for sale. Dorica was as much part of Brian's world as she was mine.

Dorica and Brian shared different interests than she and I did. He loved to be at home with her. I liked going places and having fun in nature. Dorica gave me the perfect excuse to take picnics, have barbecues, and go on long walks. We would climb exercise equipment on the playground. She loved moving and challenging herself.

We made every outing special. We loved the beaches and climbing on old railroad cars. We found endless opportunities to move around. At home she would drag books and stuffed bears around. She constantly begged me to read to her, play with her, do puzzles, and talk to the many bears she lined up.

Our life seemed idyllic in one sense, but the stress over the years took its toll. Between our busy professional lives and responsibilities at home, Brian and I had very little time to enjoy each other without Dorica. We worked hard and devoted all of our resources to creating a stable life for her. Dorica required our attention twenty-four hours per day.

We could scarcely afford the luxury of a babysitter, but even still we tried training several. Dorica presented formidable challenges to retaining any of them, no matter how good they were: She required overnight care. She wore diapers that needed changing. Unable to speak in sentences, she could not express herself. Because she could not understand why we were gone, she would wander outside trying to find us—even at night. Most of the caregivers we hired quit after one night. That left no time for the two of us on evenings and weekends. Without ever acknowledging it to each other, we began to drift apart.

As things go, the symptom often parades as the cause. Brian needed to attend the yearly consumer electronic show in Las Vegas, and he asked me to accompany him. I had to teach school. Even if we could have afforded it, we knew that hiring anyone to stay with Dorica for a week would end in disaster. He needed me as his wife. I had no choice but to stay behind.

About six months before the electronics show, Brian had hired an assistant to help him. She answered the phone, helped him with paperwork, and handled customer service. She went to Las Vegas in my place. And ultimately, she took my place. They may have consummated their relationship on that trip, but ours had started to fall apart well beforehand.

Another issue had driven a wedge in our relationship: Brian wanted a second child. I was adamantly opposed. What if we had another special needs child? We didn't know the origin of Dorica's condition and whether one of us possessed a genetic predisposition. He wanted another sibling to support Dorica. I didn't want to take the chance. We wanted different things. We found ourselves drifting apart.

I did not fault Brian when he fell for his assistant. It certainly hurt, but on some level it did not surprise me. From the moment she came into the picture, she supported Brian in caring for Dorica. She herself took on caregiving responsibilities. I could tell she was an honorable person. Brian had been a wonderful husband. And while I struggled with the difficulty of letting such a good man go, I wished him well so he could find the happiness he sought. To this day, I remain friends with this very fine woman.

Brian and I divorced on amicable terms. We made a commitment that we would always share Dorica's care, that we would never neglect her, and that we would never let her suffer. And while I initially questioned whether Brian would keep his word, he quickly demonstrated his commitment. We both kept our promises over the years.

Despite the challenges of the circumstance, I saw it as an opportunity to recreate my life. I had a secure job, and I knew I could manage Dorica's care with Brian's help. We still remained a team. It gave me solace that Brian's new girlfriend fully accepted and welcomed Dorica.

Brian and his new girlfriend married, and then on February 28, 1992, when Dorica was twenty-four years old, they had a girl named Terra. Dorica gained the sibling that Brian had long wanted for her. Brian raised Terra as Dorica's sister, and from the beginning, the two became inseparable. To this day, Terra displays incredible caring and understanding for Dorica, and the two of them complement each other. In the end, Brian created a stronger support structure for Dorica than I could ever imagine.

Even though Dorica stayed at Brian's place just every other weekend, Terra acted protectively toward Dorica. I could not feel more blessed. Brian's wife was kind and caring toward Dorica as well. We often said that we were one big family. For me, life actually became a little easier since I could do other things on the weekends while Dorica was gone.

Dorica adjusted to these changes like a champ. As long as she had food, a bed, and music somewhere, she was content. Her loving family had grown, she was enjoying the adult care center she attended, and she had her mother almost totally to herself. How much better could it get?

Well, it got even better. And it was Dorica who paved the way—she became a matchmaker.

It happened on one of our weekend outings in a park. I was pushing her in her wheelchair while we both admired the nature around us. She uttered some of the few words she knows and touched the trees.

A gentleman noticed how much we enjoyed each other. He followed us and introduced himself before we got to the parking lot. He told us how beautiful it was to see such love, gentleness, and joy pass between two people, and he asked if he join us. That is how I met my second husband Howard.

I never expected to meet someone so soon, and marriage was the furthest thing from my mind, especially since I had a handicapped child. Yet, a year after my divorce, Howard showed up in my life.

Howard also had a daughter, almost the same age as Dorica but already living on her own. He too was divorced, and his ex-wife had remarried. When we began courting, he would accompany me on fieldtrips with my students on the weekends when Dorica stayed with her father. He and I would build telescopes with the students on Friday nights. We would teach them hydroponics and other science lessons at the Lawrence Livermore Lab.

Howard did the things with me that were not on Brian's radar. He loved working on construction projects and as an engineer. He helped my school by wiring the classrooms for Internet access. Howard liked Dorica, and she accepted him from the beginning. Soon she had him wrapped around her finger. It was amazing to see how she could make him feel loved, liked, and accepted. Howard needed this kind of love and acceptance, and he enjoyed being needed and helpful.

Howard and I fell in love with each other and began to make plans. We married after a year. Yes, love can strike more than once. I felt so fortunate. We started traveling, which Brian made possible because he kept Dorica when we were gone. Brian and I never had this luxury even when we tried our best to go together and travel.

Dorica and Howard became a team. He started teaching her good manners, such as pouring milk into a glass instead of drinking it out of a carton. She waited for food instead of grabbing it. She became very polite and amazingly ladylike, saying "please" and "thank you."

She loved Howard's gentlemanlike attitude, and it rubbed off on her. She began to insist on dressing decently, which came as a complete surprise to me. She even started putting her toys and records in order before she left the house. Howard's example inspired these and other subtle changes in her.

Because she liked Howard so much, Dorica accepted Howard as part of our team. At times that meant following his directives. He never had to raise his voice, and he always respected her. They inherently understood each other. If we went to a restaurant, a displeasing look from him would stop her from becoming a nuisance. He would always praise and hug her when she behaved well.

But then one morning, eight years after we married, tragedy struck. I found Howard on the floor of his favorite room—the den—dead, at only sixty-one years old. Congestive heart failure. He had been having difficulty breathing, and the night before he told me he felt incredibly tired.

I knew he had had a heart condition, but this came as a tremendous shock. "Why now?" I asked the universe, "What will become of Dorica and me?" We traveled around the world together. Howard complemented me in so many ways. He was my intellectual equal, and we approached ideas and life's mysteries with equal curiosity. He maintained the house impeccably—constantly repairing and building things—so I never had to worry. He taught Dorica manners and discipline in a gentle, kind way. And yet even in my shocked state, I knew this happened for a reason.

I let him lie on the floor for a few hours after I found him. His spirit would need time to make a smooth transition to the next realm, and the sudden movement of his body could cause him confusion. He needed to get his bearings in the spirit world. In these few hours, we said our goodbyes to our shared embodied experience and settled into a new way of connecting with each other.

The next day Howard came to me insistently—he wanted me to conduct a fire ceremony to help ease his transition to the spirit world. I listened. In the fireplace that he had built—inspired by our trip to India—I lit a fire and conducted the ceremony. I felt his presence and appreciation for my efforts. The connection we shared helped me move through my grief. I knew I could always call on him.

In true Howard fashion—always one to be kind and considerate—Howard had left me suddenly so he would not become a burden. He knew I had my hands full with Dorica. He created beautiful things in my life, and we had loved each other dearly. We had completed our time together.

Dorica responds to loss with an amazing sense of non-attachment—she's generally unfazed when people leave and things disappear. Yet, when people return—no matter how many years later—she will remember them immediately and pick up where they left off. Howard's passing was no different. She keeps his legacy alive by still pouring milk into a glass, being as polite and gentle as he taught her, and always expressing the highest level of loving kindness. It is like he is still here watching over her.

On December 12, 2012, Dorica's father Brian passed away from cancer. Since his death, Terra has taken his place in Dorica's heart. She regularly brings Dorica home with her so she can listen to music in the sound room with Brian's old loudspeakers. When Terra arrives, I can see the love in both of their faces. Brian lives on through Dorica's love for music.

Dorica stuns us at times, for she will speak Brian's name as if he were present. I know he watches over her. In fact, Dorica has gained two allies in the spirit world—Brian and Howard.

It took almost a whole village to raise and care for Dorica. She is now fifty-one years old and has good people surrounding her. When she was thirty-eight, she was fortunate to have been accepted at a supportive Board-and-Care home, Ventura Hills

Manor, where she lives and sleeps during the week. Of course, she is the sweetheart of the whole place—she makes friends so easily. On weekends she still comes home to me. She also attends the Hilltop Adult Center on weekdays for therapies and support. As always, she has mastered the art of making friends with the staff and clients.

Chapter 3

DORICA'S UNUSUAL GIFTS

Dorica wants to help me prepare a meal—potato soup, one of her favorites. We wash the potatoes. I guide her hands so she holds the knife properly. We cut and count the pieces, kiss each one, and say hello to them. We sing a song to the potato pieces, dance around them, and say goodbye as we throw them into the pot.

Dorica intently watches the potatoes as they cook—she wants to make sure they are happy. She waits patiently as I ladle the soup into bowls, quietly honoring the soul of the food in a way that resembles prayer. She offers me the first spoonful.

In Dorica's world, a simple task becomes a precious gift. A meal becomes something to celebrate. With wisdom that arises from sources beyond my knowing, Dorica teaches me about life in so many ways.

For example, Dorica loves nature. She notices trees, bushes, flowers, rocks, and grass—and not just visually. She tunes into their energy and communes with them. When we go to parks on the weekends, we have to—*have to*—stop at certain trees. She reaches for their branches, shakes them, says hello, and then waits for a response. She has a few favorite trees, which she will get up from her wheelchair to greet. She'll hug them and give their bark a big kiss.

She connects with the spirits of the trees like a shaman, drawing from their energy and giving back to them in kind. When she's done, she bids them goodbye with laughs and smiles. She makes a ceremony of it.

Sometimes she'll lie down on a grassy field and gaze at the sky. She reads the clouds like a text, as if she understands what they are telling her. I've learned to leave her alone at times like these. Even if I try, nothing will disturb her—dogs, helicopters, nor anything else. She'll remain completely still in an intense, wordless state of connection with the clouds, which can last for more than a half-hour.

I'll know she has returned to her body when she begins moving her hand and arm back and forth on the grass, gently and lovingly, touching and communicating with each blade. When she comes back from the clouds, her face often appears clear, serious, and knowing, like a wise woman—different from when she communes with the trees.

Because Dorica loves plants and trees so much, I bought her a houseplant—a philodendron, which has long hanging vines and large leaves. I placed it on the bookshelf above her bed. Every night before she goes to sleep, she touches the leaves with her hands and gently strokes them with her arm. Like she does with trees and grass, she creates a ceremony when she connects with this plant. I don't know where she learned this, as I did not teach it to her.

The plant seems to appreciate it. It sends its vines down just above her head, perfect for her to stroke, but never close enough to bother her at night. Even with my sporadic watering, the plant seems very happy.

Dorica's ability to connect with the essence of plants and nature echoes the writings of the spiritualist Malidoma Patrice Somé, who hails from the Dagara tribe in West Africa. Somé describes how his people view the spiritual realms:

> *In the culture of my people, the Dagara, we have no word for the supernatural... In Western reality, there is a clear split between the spiritual and the material, between religious life and secular life. This concept is alien to the Dagara. For us, as for many indigenous cultures, the supernatural is part of our everyday lives. To a Dagara man or woman, the material is just the spiritual taking on form.*[1]

Dorica can connect with the spiritual realms in ways that most of us cannot. I suspect that she senses the aura of plants and tunes into their energy signal when she rubs her hands and arms across them. She models a totally different way of relating to plants.

Her love of nature inspired me to start a butterfly garden so I could surround her with more wildlife. When she sits in the garden, bees, butterflies, and hummingbirds buzz around. Her face lights up and she begins to laugh when she sees a bee land on a flower. She has never received a single sting, not even from a mosquito. It's magic. Watching her reminds me of my childhood when I was more tuned into nature, and it serves to remind me to maintain that connection in my daily life.

Dorica's strong connection to the plant world would lead one to expect she would have a similar connection to animals. Special children seem to share a love for animals as well as plants. This is not the case for Dorica, and it has always puzzled me.

Dorica grew up with pets. Her father loved calicos, and we always had one or two in the house. We took care of a neighbor's dog for a while. We had two canaries for years, which flew

---

[1] Nick Polizzi, *Soul Wisdom from the Dagara Tribe*, http://www.thesacredscience.com/soul-wisdom-from-the-dagara-tribe/, accessed October 9, 2017.

freely around the house. We had an aquarium with fish. We had a turtle. Dorica expressed absolutely no interest in any of them. And it seemed that the animals felt similarly toward her—they kept their distance. Now we have no pets in the house, which seems to suit Dorica just fine.

One time a cat tried to cozy up to Dorica. She rubbed her head on Dorica's lap and purred. Wrong move. Dorica grabbled the cat by the tail and held it in the air for a while, clearly communicating her boundaries. The cat never tried that again. Dorica is never cruel to animals—she just tells them to leave her alone.

Dorica is not afraid of animals, and she is friendly to dogs in the park that greet her. But most animals sense that she is somehow different. They behave gently and with curiosity toward her, wanting to engage but not certain how. They usually accept her and leave her alone, and she does likewise.

How Dorica Relates to People—and How People Relate to Her

To most people, the idea of a developmental disability seems tragic. But when people meet Dorica, this expectation gets turned upside down. Rather than feel sorry for her, people end up feeling uplifted by her. In her nonverbal way, Dorica radiates pure love. She is always smiling. She helps people forget about their troubles and redirects their energy toward joy. She heals people. The people around her forget about her disability because she makes them feel so much happier.

Dorica loves to be around people. In fact, she thrives on being the center of attention. If people ignore her, she'll shove a plush bear or stuffed animal in front of them, which means, "Talk to the bear (or animal), and play with me!" Even though she cannot really talk, she expresses a certain striking humor. Her whole body says, "Playtime!" She lacks the inhibitions most of us have, which disarms people, relaxes them, and helps them have fun.

She has an uncanny ability to read people's authenticity. When she meets someone for the first time—male or female—she scans the person intensely and with complete focus. People have commented that they feel as though she reads their past, present, and future lives quite rapidly. When someone passes the test, Dorica breaks out into a big smile and embraces that person.

From that point on, Dorica gives unconditional love. Once she knows a person's character, she'll forgive just about any flaw—even getting angry. If you do get angry, she just waits for you to calm down.

On the other hand, if you don't pass her character test, Dorica will tell you. Once I had a male guest at my home who Dorica felt uneasy about. She took his hand, led him out the door, and said "good-bye" as she shoved him outside. I apologized to him, but I knew enough to trust Dorica's judgment. Later I learned that this man had a history of uncontrolled anger and abuse. Somehow, on some level, Dorica knew this.

Living with Dorica's propensity to turn people away is not easy at times. I have found, however, that her ability to gauge whether someone will have a positive or negative influence on us is always accurate. She will accept people, even depressed ones, as long as they have a good heart and soul. She pays no mind to a person's color, the clothes they wear, their position in life, or their mannerisms.

For example, not long ago we were walking in a park and Dorica moved in her wheelchair on the wrong side of the path. Another woman, also in a wheelchair, wheeled past us and reprimanded Dorica for being on the wrong side. There was enough space for both. Dorica said "hi" to her, when she started saying something that she wanted to let the police know that we were on the wrong side. What? I started laughing and Dorica started laughing and that made the woman even more angry. Dorica just smiled and we kept on going.

The next week, the same woman came by and we moved early enough to the correct side. This time Dorica tried to make friends and touched her arm with her hand while passing. Wrong move. The woman started yelling at Dorica. Dorica started laughing again and me too. We let it go.

The third time we met the woman Dorica had the nerve to start singing a lullaby song. For the first time, the woman started smiling and even said "Hello." We all smiled. The problem was solved. Dorica found the key: music.

Dorica understands there's always a way to touch someone's heart. I believe that all special children have much keener perceptions of character than we give them credit for. They see through the appearances that distract most of us and perceive an individual's essence. It is stunning and very genuine.

If Dorica feels she is not being treated properly, she will communicate her feelings unequivocally. She is so gentle and loving that she literally won't accept harshness, rudeness, or meanness—she'll hold her ears when this happens. In this way she serves as a mirror for bad behavior. It stops people in their tracks—they don't expect it, and it makes them realize what they are doing.

She also has firm boundaries and lets people know when they cross a line. If she feels a request is not reasonable, she will tell you and let you know her response is final.

A Special Friend

When Dorica has less control over a situation in which she feels she's being mistreated, she finds ways to enlist others to help her. One time a bus driver in her day care program was treating her harshly. He would push her around jerkily in the wheelchair and speak loudly to her. In response, Dorica became very agitated.

But there was also a blind man riding the bus and he helped her.

Recognizing she was upset about the situation, he took her hand and talked softly to her. He urged her to cooperate with the bus driver because her agitation would only make things worse. This calmed her down, and she agreed to try to get along better with the bus driver. Without telling Dorica, he spoke with staff at the facility about the incident. Two days later, they removed the bus driver. I had to smile because she found someone else speak up for her.

Dorica will listen to this man when nobody else can calm her. He is quite verbal and expressive. He looks out for Dorica and treats her gently. They have managed to maintain a close friendship for more than thirty years. He keeps me apprised of things about her that I need to know, which is a great gift to me. I find it amazing how they complement and support each other despite their different limitations. While they genuinely care for each other, they remain platonic friends. Neither crowds the other. They simply enjoy each other's company.

I believe that if the world had more special ones, we would have fewer wars and less abuse. Dorica holds everyone to high standards of behavior—gentleness, compassion, caring, and support. The world could certainly benefit from more of us living up to those standards.

Dorica Meets the Lamas

Knowing that Dorica often went to church with her father's family and was accustomed to listening to the choir and church music, I took her to a performance of the Guyoto Monks at a high school in my area. I wondered what would happen when she heard the sounds of the instruments and the chants. It was quite something to watch her.

Something about the monks' music affected her in a profoundly different way. As soon as they started chanting and playing, Dorica's whole body began to shake. I thought it might be too much for her. Then she settled into a rhythm, moving her body back and forth, shaking her arms and legs. Her whole body became motion, like water. She started singing with the chants as if she knew the melodies. She seemed transported to another universe, totally at ease.

Fortunately we were in a large high school auditorium, so Dorica did not disturb anyone. As soon as the music and chants stopped, Dorica stopped. She returned to her body, her old self.

Another time I brought her to meet one of the holy Lamas, a Tibetan monk and member of the Dalai Lama's entourage that was visiting Berkeley. The Lama blessed her by touching her head with his finger, which he held there for a long time. As he did this, Dorica's whole body started shivering, and happiness spread across her face. She remained in this shivering state for the entire blessing. It was stunning to witness.

These experiences led me to research shamanic trance states. I wondered if Dorica had entered into such trances through these means. In the booklet *Shamans of the 20th Century*, Ruth-Inge Heinze writes:

> Techniques to go into trance differ considerably. Some shamans use meditation in solitude, some require drumming and chanting in public. Achterberg reports that the sound of the percussion instruments and the rattles are time-honored methods for consciousness altering, and are considered to have a numbing or analgesic effect. Sound, traveling on the pathways of the brain stem, is capable of activating the entire brain. Other sensory stimuli from ordinary reality…could be gated or filtered out. The mind would then be free to expand into other realms.[2]

Sometimes shamanic trance states can lead to the kind of full-body shaking I observed in Dorica. It is also possible that the monks' chanting and playing, and the holy Lama's touch activated Dorica's Kundalini energy, something Tantric Zen practitioners describe. Either way, it seems that Dorica—and many special children—enter trances and other states of consciousness more readily than most of us. They have a closer connection to spiritual realms.

---

2   Ruth-Inge Heinze, *Shamans of the Twentieth Century*, (Berkeley: University of California, Berkeley, Irvington Publishers, 1991), 94.

Terra

From the moment Dorica's half-sister, Terra, was born, Dorica gained a buddy. The two bonded very early on and have always maintained a close relationship. Terra is a kind, gentle, compassionate, and free spirit. She understands Dorica and would defend her with her life.

When Terra was young, some of her friends would often make fun of Dorica, but Terra would have none of it. She even got into fights to defend her sister. As Terra matured, despite having her own life and school activities, she occasionally picked up Dorica from my house to take her on special Sunday outings. She continued this even after their father died.

Terra shared this about her relationship with Dorica:

> Dorica has always been in my life. I never had to adjust to her—she had to adjust to me, being in her late twenties when I was born. From my earliest childhood memories, I remember always having a deep, passionate love for my sister. To everyone who didn't know Dorica, she was different, and they were curious about her. For me, she was just my sister. It never occurred to me to ask why she is the way she is. I just knew her as Dorica. And I loved her.
>
> My father had Dorica stay with us every other weekend. Because she was around so much, we developed a close relationship. I remember when my parents would buy lunch. I would bring it down to her, set us up on a little table, and sit with her and eat. It was our "thing" to do.
>
> We played with stuffed animals together, but what really got her excited was flipping through magazines. She would point at the pictures and name what she saw. "Doggy!" she'd say and smile at me. "Good job Dorica! Doggy," I'd respond. "Now what's this one?" And if she didn't know, of course I'd teach her what it was and she'd

repeat it. Every night when she went to bed, I'd read her her favorite book, *Maisy Goes to Bed*, and she would laugh and smile. The joy that fills her eyes as you interact with her is so beautiful and breathtaking. She wants so little, to just be loved and cared for, just like the rest of us. I've always been so passionate about Dorica and how much she means to me.

My father would take us bowling on the weekends she came over. She loved to watch people play, and sometimes she would crawl to the lane herself and push the ball down. Oh, the excitement on her face watching a bowling ball knock down pins!

With Dorica's condition, she walks slowly and usually needs to hold onto something or somebody. One time I remember helping her walk into the bowling alley with my childhood best friend. I was probably about nine years old. We were slowly making our way to our lane and Dorica held onto me as I helped her walk. As we approached our lane, I noticed a group of boys around my age pointing and laughing. I became instantly angry. My best friend told me to ignore them.

One of the bullies walked up to Dorica and me. "Keep it up. You're. Doing. A. Gooood job," he said mockingly as he turned to his friends. They all laughed. Nothing pisses me off more than someone speaking to my sister like she's stupid. I cornered the boy and yelled, "Don't make fun of my sister!" and punched him in the face. I'd like to think my dad purposely looked away with a little joy for my standing up for her.

Growing up with a special needs family member is truly eye opening. Even as a child, I would get upset when someone made fun of or mistreated the special needs kids at my school. I intervened many times because people mistreated them. I felt strongly that I could not let that injustice happen.

Taking care of Dorica isn't easy. And I don't mean that in a bad way. She's much like a toddler. You have to feed her, bathe her, dress her, and walk with her. She sometimes throws tantrums. But truthfully, I actually loved taking care of her. I would bathe her. I would rub lotion on her and dress her. I would change her diapers and brush her hair. It felt great to take care of her and help out. I know my parents and her mother appreciated it too, but I simply felt joy being able to love her.

One might think my relationship with Dorica's mother—my father's ex-wife—would be awkward, but it's anything but that. Astrid and I have always loved each other. She has told me my entire life how much she appreciates me and how much I love Dorica. Astrid and I grew close when I was about ten years old. I often went to her house for dinner, and she would tutor me. We would eat and laugh with Dorica. It was beautiful, really.

It's ironic that what society sees as an "incompetent" or "challenged" human being is actually a wonderful, loving, special person who brought our family together. She's taught all of us so much. Dorica has made me the person I am today—patient, open-minded, and compassionate. She's the reason Astrid and I have a great relationship.

That's what's so special about her—she brings people together. She is the reason for this family's compassion, kindness, and understanding. I would never wish to change her. My sister is a blessing to the world and no one can ever tell me otherwise. I'm so thankful for her being in my life.

—Terra Cheney, 2016

Dorica's Many Interests

Despite the fact that she has difficulties standing or walking, Dorica likes moving, exercising, and especially dancing. One of her knees bends outward, which causes her to tilt to one side. She can walk slowly with a walker, but short distances at the most. She can crawl or walk on her knees faster—and she often prefers doing so. Most of the time she needs a wheelchair. Notwithstanding these physical limitations, "let's go" is one of her favorite expressions.

There is nothing slow about her. In fact, she is the one who gets me, her mother, moving. She wakes up with the birds while I want to sleep forever. She turns the TV channel to *Easy Yoga* and moves with the instructor. She says "bike" and proceeds to our rowing machine. She says "walk" and heads out the door with her walker. She crawls up and down our hallway on her knees. She turns her music on and rocks and dances. This could go on all day if I let her.

She always wants me to exercise with her. It's great fun to match her innate rhythm. I can't complain—I hardly go out dancing anymore. Dorica gives me plenty of joy, fun, and exercise.

Even though she cannot talk, Dorica is a very social being. She loves picnics, big barbecues, and playground crowds. She enjoys having fun with people. I have no idea where she learned all this. It's fine, though: A mother does not need to know everything.

There's another incongruous side to Dorica's personality: For as gentle and loving a being as she is, she loves violent, bloody movies. They make her laugh, in fact. The more screaming and blood, the better. She also loves watching Wrestle Mania. It might be that Brian and Terra went to scary movies with her, but I am just guessing.

I mostly avoid violent movies, as they give me nightmares. The scenes become imprinted on my mind, and I can struggle for years to rid myself of them. I cannot stand the phoniness of wrestling either, coupled with its violence.

Dorica seems unaffected by violence in movies and wrestling, however. She seems to know it is not real. I've studied her after she watches violent movies, and I haven't been able to detect any change or imprint on her soul. She could watch a robot rip a dog to shreds on screen, and laugh. Later at home she'll be as gentle as always with her stuffed dogs.

It makes me marvel: She can distinguish between reality and illusion and let the illusion go. She teaches me even when she watches movies.

Dorica's Healthy Instincts

Some years ago I realized that Dorica instinctively gravitated to foods that kept her healthy. For instance, I noticed that she developed a preference for organic produce. She would refuse to eat any vegetables that had been conventionally grown. If I gave her carrots, she would eat the organic carrot and reject the conventionally grown one. The same went for apples and potatoes. I don't know how she discerned the difference—was it taste, smell, texture? Whatever the reason, I switched to buying organic produce only. Fortunately, we now have farmers' markets that offer many organic choices.

My neighbors know about Dorica's preferences and help me out by bringing vegetables from their gardens, apples from their backyards, oranges for fresh-squeezed juice, and much, much more. My Latino neighbors bring me tamales, tacos, and corn chips that they prepare by hand from fresh ingredients at home. We talk, we are laughing, and we share wisdom, knowledge, and resources. Food nourishes our bodies, and our community nourishes our souls. Dorica once again became our teacher, facilitating this more healthful approach to living. After we switched to organic food, Dorica went for two years without having a cold, flu, or any other illness.

She also knows how to use food to heal herself. Since Dorica was a small child, she has liked to eat lemons—rind, peel, and all. Since I have a lemon tree in the garden, we always have a supply of organic lemons. Dorica will eat one lemon on and off all day.

A few years ago, Dorica received a vaccination at school. The next day, she began to sniffle and looked lethargic. She started rummaging around the kitchen, and I recognized that she was looking for a lemon, so I gave her one. She ate it in one sitting, and had nothing else all day long. The next day, whatever had ailed her was gone. She resumed eating other foods and felt fine.

Later I learned about some of the potential side effects of the flu vaccine, which can include digestive problems, joint and muscle pains, aches, and lethargy, among others. Among other ingredients, the vaccine contains thiomersal, a preservative and form of mercury. I also learned that lemon peels are loaded with Vitamin C, minerals, and potassium, and that eating them detoxifies cells and reduces oxidation. In retrospect, I realized that Dorica instinctively knew what could help clear toxins from her system and reduce the vaccine's side effects.

Dorica and Music

Earlier, I shared about Dorica's love of music. Now I will tell you why.

Music has always been part of her life. Her father surrounded her with music from the time she was born, and her half-sister continued that tradition. Dorica developed her own taste over time, however. For instance, Christmas music is one of her favorites. So I get to hear Christmas songs year-round! She plays *Jingle Bells* constantly on the Record Player.

A few years ago, she found a musical instrument at Walgreens—a ring with bells attached. She *had* to have it. Now, when she plays *Jingle Bells* I hear actual bells accompany the music. Now that she lives in a Board-and-Care home during the week, when she returns to me on the weekends, our house becomes a sound chamber of music of her choosing.

She begins playing her records on low volume as soon as the birds start singing in the morning. When the music plays, Dorica enters her own world, and she does not like being bothered or interrupted. This is fine with me, as it gives me two to three hours of extra time to sleep.

Later, when I get up, she'll turn up the volume and sing with the songs. Imagine this scene: The record player blasting, bells shaking, and Dorica singing and sometimes dancing. Given her nearly nonverbal state, I find this totally amazing. She rocks to the music, dances with it, and sings with it. The music makes her feel free. I would never want to stop or restrict this pure expression of joy.

Fortunately, she has other favorites besides Christmas carols. She likes *101 Dalmations*—I bet she knows every line on the record. I hear her trying to imitate the words or sounds without knowing the meaning of what they say or sing. She has records with dogs and wolfs howling and I hear her howling like a wolf accompanying the record. She listens to Ernie and Bert, other *Sesame Street* songs, organ music, blues, Zumba, dance music, and more.

I don't know exactly how many records she has—at least 300. She recognizes every record by its label. She will go through 150 of them, throwing them all over the room until she finds the one she wants to hear. She chooses very deliberately. Trying to influence her decision will not work—she will immediately remove my choice if she does not want to hear it.

Interestingly, it turns out that Dorica can distinguish between her analog records and digital recordings. I found this out a few years ago when her day care center bought her an iPad and loaded some of her favorite songs on it. She did not like the sound quality of digital music. She tried to be polite and listen, but then she would walk away.

An esoteric teacher of mine once commented that digital audio actually "misses" some of the sounds because it cuts them out, whereas analog presents a more a complete sound. Clearly, Dorica hears this difference and prefers silence to incomplete music.

Dorica is in many ways a perfectionist. If she has any control over her choices, she will seek perfection. For example, when she pours a glass of water, she will go to extra lengths to make sure she pours it smoothly and does not spill a drop. I can see the change in her face when she thinks she has fallen short. For Dorica, choosing the music she wants to hear gives her control over her environment. The joy this gives her makes the occasional broken record and needle replacement a small price to pay.

Even though she loves listening to music so much, she joyfully engages in other activities during the day. It amazes me that she never gets upset when it is time to stop what she's involved with and do something else. I really could learn from her.

Dorica and the Spirit of All Things

Dorica never cared for dolls, despite having received many as gifts. She would either ignore or throw them away. Instead, she gravitated toward her stuffed furry bears and other animals.

To this day, four stuffed animals travel with us in the car. Before we leave the house, we have to pet a particular stuffed hairy bird and press a knob on it to hear a sound from the bird. While I initially thought this was Dorica's way of simply saying goodbye to this bird, the persistence of this behavior over time—she never neglects doing so, no matter how hurried we are—made me realize it is a ritual. Before we get into the car, she connects with our protective spirit bird and higher beings, asking them in her own way to keep us safe.

And they do: I have never had an accident with Dorica in the car. Dorica always reminds me not to leave without our allies. As in so many other ways, Dorica serves as my teacher and protector.

Dorica sees her world as a playground. Everything—from talking to bears, to cooking in the kitchen or enjoying nature—is a game for her. She is fully present in the moment. It is fun to watch her.

The stuffed animals have a soul; she talks to them. The plants have a soul; she talks to them. The veggies have a soul; she talks to them. The records have a soul; she talks to them. Whether she encounters people, birds, plants, soil, or rocks, she engages them fully. She treats them equally, as if she understands that they all have a spirit.

Stones, too, seem to hold some magic for Dorica. She loves them, and often picks one up on our outings. She will touch the stone, rub it, say "hi" to it, and rub it some more. We often take one home, and now a whole collection of stones sits on the windowsill. She washes them. We even play with them at times, giving them names or even painting them. She will show me when she wants to play with them.

It is not just play, however. We create circles out of them. We sing and talk to them. The stones seem to have a soul—they are as real as live beings for her. Interestingly, she will not collect or interact with manmade concrete. She just ignores it.

I wanted to understand why Dorica has such an affinity for stones, so I did some research. I discovered that ancient cultures worshipped stones. For instance, ancient Jewish tradition recognized sacred stones, with the belief that deities lived within them. This belief spread throughout the ancient world and was adopted among the Greeks and Romans.[3] The ancients, of course, erected massive temples using stone—Stonehenge and the Egyptian pyramids being some of the most well known— whose purposes still remain mysterious today.

For Hindus, the lingam stone, a stylized phallus, represents masculinity and the masculine force in creation. The yoni stone represents matter and energy, sky god and earth mother. Together they represent the fertile union that created the universe.

Dorica treats stones as living, energetic objects—something the ancients recognized. Once again, she seems to possess a connection with other realms that most of us have either forgotten or simply cannot access.

---

[3] Emil G. Hirsch and Immanuel Benzinger, "Stone and Stone-Worship," *The Jewish Encyclopedia*, accessed February 2, 2018, http://www.jewishencyclopedia.com/articles/14059-stone-and-stone-worship.

A Presence in Our Neighborhood

In a way that defies easy explanation, Dorica's presence in our neighborhood has brought peace and happiness to it. After we moved in, more and more compassionate, caring people followed suit. Even a Tibetan Buddhist Temple built a center not ten minutes from our house.

It might seem a coincidence, but I think it's more than that. Dorica's presence radiates love, and everyone who meets her falls under her spell. Even before they meet her, visitors to our cul-de-sac can sense the harmonious energy that abounds here. Dorica is our neighborhood's avatar.

When we first looked at the house, I felt drawn to it for the safety the cul-de-sac would provide Dorica. I brought Dorica to see it, and she immediately made her way to the garden, touching the flowers. She looked happy, and I knew this would make a good place to put down some roots. Dorica did the rest of the work.

During our first years living here, we found a stone statue of Buddha in a nursery. Dorica touched its head over and over again, and did not want to leave it. We took that as a sign to buy it, and we placed it in the garden. I believe it became our protective statue, radiating good energy around us.

Three years later a spring emerged from beneath the Buddha statue, which gives us water for months every year. How did this happen? The water created a channel between our house and the house next door, disturbing nobody. All of us—our next-door neighbor, Dorica, Howard, and I—began caring for the spring, creating gardens on either side. The spring appears every fall and winter during the rainy season and dries out in the summertime. Birds come to drink and bathe in it. Dorica loves to touch the running water and finds it an endless wonder.

Two years later we started planting trees. A now-big apple tree gives us fresh apples for months and gave Dorica branches to swing and hang on. Slowly the garden became a peaceful oasis, where people loved to come. We have hosted many fire ceremonies, talks, and get-togethers in the garden. Dorica's love for nature, and her ability to communicate with the plants that grow in our garden, helped us create a sacred space that became the glue for our little community.

Our neighbors share a common care and concern for each other and the earth. Some raise chickens, most tend gardens and grow vegetables. We meet and talk with each other. Newcomers feel the peaceful vibrations from the moment they arrive, and they want to be part of it. Dorica helped to create this loving feeling through the love she freely gives to everyone. Even though she's only here on weekends now, neighbors know she's here when they hear her music lofting through the air.

Chapter 4

WHO *IS* DORICA?

"Most people see what is, and never see what can be."
—Albert Einstein

Dorica and I are sitting on the living room floor silently and in stillness, gazing through the open window at the setting sun. The neighborhood is eerily quiet. No children playing, no dogs barking, no sounds of music. A warm breeze wafts through the room. Exhausted from a long day, Dorica and I slip into a meditative state.

Dorica touches my hand—she wants to show me something. Suddenly and inexplicably, I feel myself slipping into her body and her slipping into mine. A profound sense of serenity descends upon me. I can feel Dorica's thoughts, her energy, and her being. Looking next to me, I witness my body, which is now occupied by Dorica. Time ceases. I feel eternity.

As abruptly as it began, it ends. I return to my body and wonder what just happened. More than that, I ask, how on Earth did Dorica achieve this feat? Who and what is she?

I wrote that passage a few years back. Although Dorica has always demonstrated special abilities, this astonishing experience left me in a state of puzzlement and awe. I could not explain what Dorica had done, nor could I dismiss it. It had happened. Dorica had achieved something magical, almost miraculous.

The experience changed our relationship. Without ever needing to speak about it, she and I knew we were good for each other. We knew we could exchange bodies and energy imprints, and momentarily become another person.

It led me to ask deeper questions about her: How did she learn to do this? How did she do it so effortlessly? And even more, where did her soul come from? Why is she here? Why is she in my life? What is her life's mission? If she could talk, what spiritual knowledge could she impart?

I searched for literature on out-of-body experiences, but I could find nothing that explained this phenomenon. I wondered, did shamans use techniques like this to bring back souls from the spirit realms? Is this what Jesus did when he healed or brought a person back to life? Did he switch bodies and give that person his energy in order to be healed?

Dorica has capacities that seem to defy logic, and for which there are no easy explanations. In a world that sees special children as "disabled," their special capabilities can be easy to explain away. Society either fails to recognize, or minimizes, their talents. We must see these children with a different vision.

I may not have all of the answers to my questions about Dorica, but she has taught me the value in asking. Here are some of my theories.

A Highly Evolved Soul

In the Buddhist perspective, souls incarnate to learn certain lessons. The more lessons a soul successfully learns, the more evolved the soul becomes, and the closer it moves toward enlightenment. A fully evolved soul no longer needs to incarnate in a body and enters Nirvana.

One theory I propose is that Dorica and perhaps other special children are highly evolved souls. This may be Dorica's final incarnation. She may no longer need a body, evidenced by her ability to move into other realms so effortlessly. By serving her I am blessed to learn some of her wonderful qualities, like patience, compassion, integrity, love, self-determination, and forgiveness. It rubs off on me; I cannot help it.

Perhaps Dorica chose to incarnate to help others reach a higher level of consciousness. Meher Baba, a well-known guru in India, proposed just such a theory: he considered "special ones" to be advanced pilgrims on the spiritual path who have become spiritually intoxicated from direct awareness of God.

For some background, Meher Baba, known as the Compassionate Father, was born in 1894 in Poona, India. He was considered an avatar, chosen by the five Perfect Masters of Consciousness when he was nineteen to guide and serve mankind. These five masters, living in India in different places, all moved close to Meher Baba to become his spiritual guides. They trained him for seven years, after which he began his own mission and gathered disciples.[4]

Meher Baba began teaching his own message of love, compassion, and patience. He opened a school for boys, shelters for the poor, and a free hospital. He visited the West six times, first in 1931. In 1925 he chose to observe silence, dictating his messages only by an alphabet board until his death in 1969.

---

[4] For more details about Meher Baba, see *Who Is Meher Baba?* by K.K. Ramakrishnan, available at https://www.meherbabatravels.com/books/authors-of-baba-contents/k-k-ramakrishnan/. See also the e-book *The Path of Love* by the Avatar Meher Baba Trust, 2000, Sheriar Foundation, Myrtle Beach, South Carolina.

He traveled incognito and never handled money. He fasted for weeks at a time and slept for only two hours at night. Meher Baba led his disciples into lives of ever deeper selfless service. He practiced and taught endurance and hard work, and kept an even more strenuous pace when traveling. His followers gave him the title or motto "Mastery in Servitude."

Meher Baba's major work focused on the "special ones," which he called "masts." He endeavored to visit as many of them as possible, traveling thousands of miles to remote places throughout India and Ceylon. He considered them to be beacons of his message of love. He washed their feet and blessed them. He claimed that the "masts" are lights, placed over the globe to connect a grid of love beyond our dimensions of time and space.

I was able to visit the site in India, Meherabad, where Meher Baba worked and taught nonverbally for over twenty-five years. The minute I entered the area, I could feel this overwhelming love that lingers there. His sleeping hut still stands today, and when I entered it, I felt like I was being transported out of my body.

India also provides a more recent example of a society that values its special ones. In 2010 in the village of Jalandhar in the Indian state of Punjab, a boy was born with an unknown medical condition that left him with an enlarged forehead and narrow eyes. The villagers consider him to be a reincarnation of Ganesha, the Hindu god of good fortune, due to his striking resemblance to that god. They treat the boy, named Pranshu, as a divine child. Pranshu draws large crowds at the temple every week.

The boy enjoys his role as a religious figure. "My friends don't bully me at all as they believe I am Lord Ganesha," he says. "I am happy when people call me GaneshaJi."[5]

---

5   "Boy, six, is worshipped as the reincarnation of a Hindu GOD by Indian villagers after medical condition left him with enlarged head and narrow eyes," *Daily Mail*, November 8, 2016 (see page 57 for URL)

This could not differ more from how we in the West treat children with disabilities or disfigurement. The villagers honor this child's specialness. They do not see it as a flaw. They value the child and give him a special place in their culture. They praise him as gentle, loving, compassionate, and happy. People claim that this boy makes them feel happier when they touch him. We can learn from this approach about how to include special children in our own culture. They are here for a reason.

Just like Pranshu, Dorica makes people feel happier. People relax and smile when they hear her singing or when she touches them. Despite being extremely gentle, she can be incredibly strong-willed and determined. There is nothing weak about her. And as I discovered when she exchanged bodies with me, she has powers that even I cannot fully comprehend.

A Gift of Telepathy

As I've mentioned, Dorica has long been able to read people's intentions and energy imprints. She scans a person and seems to know about the person's past lives and future. In India, this is called accessing the Akashic Records. She also has the uncanny ability to anticipate my intentions when I'm not even present.

For instance, in the days before cellular phones, I could not always let Dorica know when I would pick her up. I might be stuck in traffic or running late and nowhere near a telephone. She would wait for me for long periods sometimes, always knowing I would show up. She does not really have a concept of time, but she does understand that care facilities follow routines—when certain things happen, it means I should be arriving soon.

---

https://www.dailymail.co.uk/news/article-3916620/Boy-six-worshipped-reincarnation-Hindu-GOD-Indian-villagers-medical-condition-left-enlarged-head-narrow-eyes.html.

After the body-switching experience, I began to wonder: Could she read my intentions if I purposefully send her mental signals or messages? How would she respond?

I began experimenting, sending her the thought that I would pick her up in a half-hour. The caretakers at the board-and-care home later confirmed that at the time I sent her that thought, Dorica moved to the window and looked outside for me. She would not budge until I arrived. I tested this several times to make sure it was not a fluke. The caretakers started noticing Dorica's determination and pattern and would light-heartedly laugh at her. It didn't matter to Dorica. When I sent her a thought that I would arrive soon, she would assume her lookout position.

I learned that I could communicate with Dorica whenever I needed to—without a cell phone. "Buddy, I am sorry, but I cannot be there yet," I'd tell her in my mind. "The traffic is heavy." She would move from her lookout post at the window and have a bite to eat, play, or do something else. "The traffic has thinned out. I'll be right there," I'd say in my mind. She would move back to the window, even if she were in the middle of eating a cookie. I compared notes with the caretakers many times about the timing of my messages, and they would confirm Dorica's movements. Our ability to communicate like this still puzzles me, and it surprises everyone we know. It comes in very handy.

We began to expand and refine our nonverbal communication over long distances. At times she will tell me she feels sad or down, and I will send her uplifting thoughts. Sometimes I will tell her jokes or something funny. Her caretakers tell me that she will start laughing at those times for seemingly no reason. I've confirmed the timing with them. Sometimes I need some cheering up. She will send me three long kisses, which I can feel on my cheek. We don't always communicate like this, but we know we can when one of us is having a difficult day.

I learned that I must have a clear state of mind for our telepathy to work. If I have consumed alcohol or am sitting in front of a computer, I will miss her signals. One time I had a dinner date and had some wine, and I sent her a thought that I would be on my way. She did not receive the message and did not sit in her lookout perch. Similarly, when I work at a computer, my signals do not reach her. Computer monitors emit low-level radiation, which might be enough to interfere with our thought-transmissions.

I have to laugh because I almost have to live like a monk in order to have this great connection with my special child. It is a small price to pay to enjoy such a fun and mindboggling kind of communication.

When I least expect it, Dorica surprises me with another message. Not long ago, she started talking about one of my friends, who she referred to as "Left, Right." (The name came from a game she played with him.) For seemingly no reason, she started saying "Left, Right" incessantly for more than twenty minutes. I knew who she meant, and out of curiosity I called my friend. I got no answer. I called again. Still no answer. I let it go.

Well, Dorica would not let it go. For a few days she kept repeating his name. After I called several more times and got no answer, I drove over to his house. No one answered the door. His mail was overflowing. I knew something terrible had happened.

I reached out to mutual friends and no one else had heard from him either. Finally, I called hospitals in the area and learned that he had landed in one with serious kidney problems. He had been in the hospital for more than one and a half weeks in a coma and had suffered memory loss. He had regained consciousness just before we contacted the hospital, and he indicated he would like to see us. When we visited and saw Mr. Left, Right in such a vulnerable state, we decided to take him home with us to nurture him back to health.

We never would have found him had Dorica not picked up on his grave condition. What's more remarkable is that he is not even the closest friend of mine. I have known him for many years, and we see him only every three or four months. He later told me that he had a dream in the hospital in which Dorica visited his room.

Once we found him, Dorica stopped saying "Left, Right" to me. His memory started to improve from the moment Dorica touched his hand. She had done her job.

Experiences like these lead me to believe that Dorica and our special ones could be oracles—that they bring messages to us from other planes of existence. They can help us navigate our daily lives, avoid danger, and even teach us how to forgive and let go of resentment. They don't judge us, even when we act from ignorance. They model compassion and unconditional love.

Dorica has such a "clean" spirit, which I believe is the key to her extraordinary abilities. Spiritual teachers tell us that that such "cleanness"—clarity of mind, body, and spirit—is necessary to access messages from the higher self or to channel information from other planes. In the ancient world, the Delphi Oracle Priestesses would enter a deep trance to channel prophecies. I have no doubt that Dorica's pureness of spirit enables her to enter different states of consciousness just like these ancient priestesses.

Beyond Telepathy

I believe that Dorica can also affect what happens in the natural world. As I shared in the previous chapter, Dorica has a strong connection with the spirits in nature. She sees what many of us cannot see. Beyond just sensing those spirits, however, she seems to play with and even influence them.

It is as if Dorica feels the same truth in her bones. Even clouds hold a magic that she can see and generously shares with me. She likes to lie in the grass or on a blanket and watch the clouds drifting by. As her eyes focus on them, she will try to tell me something by pointing to a particular clue in the cloudscape and then saying a word like "mushroom" or "elephant." It appears as if she talks to clouds and gives them a name from our earthly environment, but it is more.

Dorica truly communicates with clouds as if they are beings. Really stunning is when she almost hypnotizes a particular cloud with an intense focus, and speaks to it in her own way, waiting for an answer. She always seems to get an answer. She will start laughing, and laughing, and laughing. Then I cannot help it, I mostly start laughing too. When she stops hypnotizing the cloud, she listens intently for a reply and will start laughing again as if she got what the cloud told her. This can go on for at least half an hour.

Deep in my bones too, I can feel the connection with the universe behind the clouds. Yet Dorica has a way of letting me know how beautiful everything around us is. A simple cloud can energize her, me and the earth under us. We blend and become one.

As I wrote earlier, I experienced this connection as a girl in Germany, when I accompanied my grandmother on evening walks through the forest. We would bask in the glow of the full moon, collecting berries, mushrooms, roots, firewood, beeswax, healing herbs and waters, sap, and much more. My grandmother never feared the forest—she reveled in it. She taught me to honor the plants and creatures that lived there. She told me stories of the fairies that lived here. I listened with fascination and felt the truth of these tales in my bones.

I feel fortunate to have had both, my grandmother and Dorica as my teachers and guides in life.

All of this leads me to the question I have often asked and with which I began this chapter: *Just who is Dorica?*

I have begun to believe that, far from being "disabled," Dorica is more "abled" than most people, and can access realms beyond what most of us can perceive. Her lack of attachment to the physical—even to her own body—and to any particular outcome, hints at a focus elsewhere. What we consider a disability may very well be the *source* of her extraordinary abilities. I believe she can access higher energies and often lives in a state of pure consciousness.

She transmits this to everyone around her. People feel it when they're around Dorica. She raises the energy wherever she goes, wards off negativity and brings beauty, clarity, and energetic cleanliness to her immediate environment. She puts people at ease and heals those around her. She shares a pureness of love that people can't help but be drawn to.

Dorica inspired me to raise the bar on my own behavior so I can live at a higher level of patience, understanding, love, acceptance, and compassion for others. I am not yet as spiritually advanced as Dorica and need more life times to get through the cycles. I am still on a path of learning.

If we pay attention to our special children, we will recognize that they heal and restore us. They hold the energies we need in our lives. Indigenous peoples and ancient religious traditions use shamanism and ceremonies to access helping energies and spirits. But I think we have our own teachers right here—our special ones—who can connect us to these same realms and opportunities for healing.

We tend to see the limitations in our special children because of what their bodies cannot do. We call them "disabled." These limitations, however, may just be what give them access to what we cannot see. It may be that the abilities "normal" people possess prevent them from being able to tap into those other realms. It truly begs the question: *Just who is abled, and who is disabled?*

By writing this book, I hope to help create a world that values our special children more. I envision a time when society gives special children the recognition they deserve and allows them to fully express their gifts. Far too often they experience bullying, ridicule, and harassment. Society shuns them. This ill treatment reflects our ignorance more than anything else. To truly value special children, we must learn about their world. When we pay attention, they will challenge, surprise, and delight us.

The next two chapters provide practical suggestions for teachers, parents, and educators, based on what I've learned on how to care for special children.

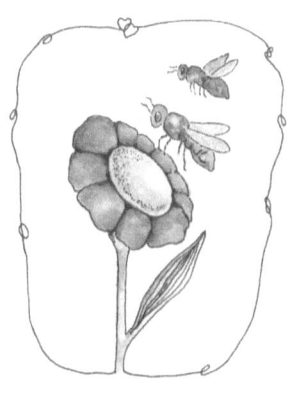

Chapter 5

PRACTICAL SUGGESTIONS FOR PARENTS WITH SPECIAL NEEDS CHILDREN

"Part of the problem with the word 'disability' is that it immediately suggests an inability to see or hear or walk or do other things that many of us take for granted. But what of people who can't feel? Or talk about their feelings? Or manage their feelings in constructive ways? What of people who aren't able to form close and strong relationships? And people who cannot find fulfillment in their lives, or those who have lost hope, who live in disappointment and bitterness and find in life no joy, no love? These, it seems to me, are the real disabilities."
—Fred Rogers, The World According to Mister Rogers: Important Things to Remember

As the saying goes, it really does take a village to raise a child—especially one who has special needs. In this chapter, I provide practical advice for parents and caregivers, drawn from my experience as both a parent and schoolteacher.

This chapter focuses on six areas:

    A. Caring for Special Needs Children at Home
    B. Choosing the Right School Setting
    C. Navigating in the Community
    D. Transitioning to Adult Services
    E. Planning for the Future

A. Caring for Special Needs Children at Home

In some ways, parenting special needs children is no different from raising typical children. Effective parenting for any child requires knowing who that child really is, understanding his or her strengths and capacities, and adjusting one's parenting style accordingly. As parents of multiple children know, there is no one-size-fits-all approach. Still, special needs children pose distinct challenges. They require a level of attention, resources, and patience that can stretch parents beyond every limit they imagined possible.

I offer the following observations and suggestions based on what I have learned throughout my many years of caring for Dorica. Every special needs child, parent, family unit, and circumstance is different, so I suggest you adapt these suggestions to your own situation.

Creating a Support Team

No parent of a special needs child can go it alone. Your child's condition will require that you create a care support team. The professional that most parents turn to first when their child misses developmental milestones—a pediatrician—usually becomes central to that team.

A good supportive doctor is paramount for special needs children. In addition to providing medical care, doctors serve as hubs for information. They appreciate hearing what works and does not work, and they share that information with other parents and help connect parents who face similar challenges. Take time to find the right pediatrician for you and your child. He or she will become one of your most important allies.

Beyond a pediatrician, you will need specialists and nurses, and possibly a psychologist and psychiatrist. A good social worker is essential. They can provide invaluable guidance and connect you with schools, programs, entitlements, and community resources.

These professionals are part of your support team. So are the people we discuss throughout this chapter—friends, extended family, babysitters, other parents of special needs children, and members of your church, if you belong to one. I find it helpful to create a visual image in my mind of all of these people surrounding Dorica and me, sharing their love and support. It gives me gratitude.

Coping with Pressures

Your child will spend a lot of time with you and will have considerable needs. You will face decisions about his or her care that you may not always feel qualified to make. You and your mate might disagree about the best approach to take. You may often feel overwhelmed. All of this can cause considerable stress.

Remaining calm and loving during periods of stress is one of the greatest challenges of caring for a special needs child. As I discovered, getting angry with Dorica served no purpose. It simply confused her and made her feel terrible. I had to learn to put my feelings aside and address whatever situation was at hand.

Special needs children keenly respond to their parents' mental and emotional states. They tune into each parent, as well as the dynamic between the two. If parents disagree with each other, special needs children will react to that disharmony—and they may try to manipulate the situation to their advantage.

Parents often respond to the myriad pressures upon them in many ways: They might express too much control. They might correct their children too much. Or, parents might judge themselves too harshly. After all, no one has a yardstick by which to measure one's parenting. The stress and pressures can make parents feel depressed and cynical, and make them react in mean or angry ways.

Parents can deny the severity of their child's limitations to themselves and hide those facts from others. I did this when Dorica was an infant. When she didn't sit up or walk at the developmentally appropriate time, I convinced myself and told others she was a slow learner. I did not want to believe anything was wrong with her. Brian and I didn't take her to a specialist until she was one and a half years old. Denying the reality of a child's limitations might make parents feel better temporarily, but it ultimately does not serve the child's best interests.

Conversely, parents sometimes recognize abilities in their child that do not exist. Even I—who have written this book about the magic of special children—acknowledge the distinction between recognizing the overlooked talents of a special needs child and wishful thinking.

Cultivating Patience, Building Resilience

Parenting a special needs child requires incredible patience—perhaps more than you ever knew possible. There is simply no way around it. Parents can either allow patience to develop organically or they can intentionally cultivate it. I strongly advise all parents, especially younger ones who have less experience, to commit to deliberately cultivating patience.

Consider a typical scenario: Dorica needs to go to the bathroom. I know it will take her five minutes to get up and walk across the room, and I will need to help her. I could rush her by placing her in the wheelchair and pushing her to the bathroom, or I could allow her to get some exercise and express some self-determination. I decide to help her walk. I know that anything I do with Dorica requires advance planning, so I use the five minutes to contemplate and plan what we will do later. I adjust my perspective and slow down to her rhythm.

Parents of special needs children face these kinds of choices every day. Without intentionally cultivated patience, parents can respond to these kinds of circumstances with all kinds of negative and counterproductive emotions.

Consider another example: Dorica hates going to the dentist. She doesn't like anyone prying in her mouth. She fights me and fights the hygienist. She yells and spits up, making a mess of her clothes. We have had to strap her into the chair and cover her in bed sheets. Now we give her anesthesia because she simply will not cooperate.

Again, I face a choice that pits a long-term outcome against short-term inconvenience. I want Dorica to have healthy teeth. If I neglect her dental health, I neglect part of my responsibility as a parent. For this benefit, I must inflict this discomfort on Dorica and deal with her response. I choose to endure this difficulty and subject her to this upsetting experience every two to three years. I could spiral into anger and negativity, or I could just move through the circumstance with the end in mind. I choose to focus on the long-term. I summon my strength. And I breathe. This is how I have built resilience over time.

I learned these techniques from a meditation teacher. She taught me to keep my eye on the big picture and focus on the positive. Even more powerfully, she taught me how to use my breath to slow down and redirect my emotions in the midst of challenging circumstances. By focusing on my breath—and the spaces between breaths—my anger and frustration disappear. Time and space seem to change too. Before I know it, the difficult circumstance is over.

All of this is easier said than done. It helps that I have always felt a strong sense that caring for Dorica was a *mission*—a calling. Parents who successfully build resilience share this sense of mission. It gives them strength to meet their daily challenges, and the special hug or smile they receive from their child provides the reward for their hard work.

Sometimes this hard work can end fruitlessly. By definition, special needs children struggle to learn things and master tasks that typical children pick up easily. Knowing a child's capacity and understanding when persistence will be pay off versus when it will be futile becomes critical.

For instance, I spent a year teaching Dorica how to open a bottle of juice, pick up a glass, and pour the juice into the glass instead of drinking out of a bottle. When she finally mastered it, her father and I beamed from ear to ear. It was such a joy for us. I know Dorica likes to learn, and I could tell she was making progress, which is why I persisted in teaching her this skill.

At other times I abandoned my efforts to teach her new things because I recognized when she was either not interested or incapable. Dorica exhibits telltale signs to express her disinterest: She will give up or walk away. If I get too pushy, she will just ignore me and zones out.

Dorica communicates her limits gently. Other children might throw a tantrum or express themselves differently. Tune into your child. He or she will help you recognize when to persist, and when doing so will lead nowhere.

Despite the challenges their care presents, special needs children give back in many beautiful and unexpected ways. Someone once asked me, if I could change Dorica into a normal child, would I do so? There was no question in my mind; I would not change a thing. I became a better human being through my daughter. I was spared the difficulties of the typical teenage years. Dorica and I share a love and nurturing that would be impossible had she developed typically, left the nest, and become a parent herself.

The Family Unit

A strong family unit is essential to successfully raising a special needs child. But "family" can take many forms—grandparents, older siblings, special friends—not just the standard "nuclear" family unit. We need a partner we can rely on for emotional and practical support—someone who will help us raise the child and be there consistently. Most special needs children have difficulty with changes, small or large, regardless of their disability. They don't respond well to sudden changes, as they do not have reasoning skills to understand them.

Both partners provide a critical balance. Usually, each partner brings a different dimension to parenting, and children get different needs met from them. It is important for parents to nurture their individual relationship with a special needs child, to connect with the child in their own ways, and to discover what they enjoy doing together. This also takes the pressure off each parent to be everything to the child.

In my case, I was extremely fortunate to have had a wonderful husband who, after we divorced, continued to share Dorica's care. Dorica and her father developed their own shared interests. They especially loved listening to music together. They had a strong bond until the end of his life. When he was too sick to walk, they both held onto the wheelchair. When the cancer got him down, she cheered him up.

Their bond continues beyond his death. Whenever Dorica blasts her music through the house, I feel the presence of her father's spirit working through her. Brian and I played different but equally important roles in her life.

For the family unit to effectively support a special needs child, parents must work flexibly and as a team. As I discuss in Chapter 2, teamwork kept our family unit together. Brian and I chose our professions so we could care for Dorica. I became a teacher mainly so that my summers and time off would coincide with Dorica's. Brian chose to create his loudspeaker business out of our garage so he could care for Dorica at home during the day. Early on, while I attended university, Brian took the morning shift. I worked the evening shift so he could build his business. It required a lot of dedication, but we only occasionally used outside help. (See "Choosing a Babysitter" later in this chapter for more about this.) We both agreed that our most important job in life was taking care of Dorica.

The choices Brian and I made might not work for everyone. The key is that we shared a common purpose, valued each other, created plans together, and worked as a team. Caring for a special needs child requires the equal and active participation of both partners. This advice could easily apply to strengthen any marriage. We enjoyed it so much that Dorica became an excuse for Brian and me to become good partners in life.

In fact, Dorica benefited our relationship in a way we never could never have expected. Brian and I could not go out together without taking Dorica with us, so one of us would go out while the other stayed home with her. I had good, reliable girlfriends I could roam around with. He went with his buddies to exhibitions or tradeshows. We learned to radically trust each other, something many couples have difficulty doing. For us, freedom came out of the necessity to care for Dorica—an amazing and unique side benefit.

Support beyond the nuclear family can ease some of the limitations that a special needs child can place on a couple. For us, Brian's parents proved to be a wonderful addition to the family unit and a very helpful source of support. Dorica loved her Granny. We spent most Thanksgivings, holidays, and birthdays at their place. They allowed her to be the center of attention, and they secretly spoiled her by giving her candy and cookies that we were not supposed to know about. They read to her, played with her, and let her get away with things we would not allow at home.

Every family constellation is different, but typically grandparents play important, different roles. They are often mellower than parents—less strict and demanding—and they listen and accommodate more. If the dynamics of your extended family are strained, why not allow your special one to bring you together? The fact that special needs children do not respond well to interpersonal conflict is a good reason for family members to reconsider how they interact with each other.

Some special grandparents can encourage us to be silly and light-hearted. They hold a non-judgmental mirror before us, inviting us to be authentic. They don't have the same filters and inhibitions, which we have learned from years of acculturation. They help us express more of who we are, and they help us become better people. I have observed these kinds of changes in my family as well as in other families that have special ones.

Choosing a Babysitter

At some point, you will need a babysitter. Even Brian and I—who arranged our lives so we could care for Dorica ourselves—needed to rely on outside help at times. All parents have other responsibilities, and it is important to make time for yourself and your own needs. As I mention in Chapter 2, hiring a qualified babysitter can be fraught with challenges. We learned some lessons over the years, which I would like to share here.

First and most importantly, follow your gut when choosing a babysitter. Your child will need to get to know the person before you leave him or her with the sitter. Plan ahead and don't try to rush this. Observe how your child responds during and after the encounter. When you are ready to leave your child alone with the babysitter, try a short duration first, then build up to longer intervals. A special needs child might not behave like a typical child when left with a babysitter. Separation anxiety can trigger many unusual behaviors. Train your babysitter to expect the unexpected.

Before I hired the woman who became Dorica's regular babysitter, I invited her to our house. I let Dorica observe her and me drinking coffee, talking, cooking, gardening, and being friendly with each other. I paid special attention to Dorica's response to the two of us, and in particular to how she responded to the individual. I knew that Dorica would be assessing her personality and trustworthiness.

When this person passed Dorica's test, I left them alone in a room while I did other things in the house. The prospective babysitter read books and played with Dorica. I observed Dorica's mannerisms, as I knew they would tell me how the two of them got along. Then I left them alone together in the house for short periods, about twenty minutes. When this went well enough, I extended the time I spent away until I felt confident that Dorica and the woman had bonded and established a good rapport. That is when she became my daughter's babysitter. This vetting process took time but it was worth it for our sanity.

At another point, I found a babysitter who looked after children in her own home. I didn't just drop Dorica off, however. First, I accompanied her there for short periods. I observed the visitors who came and went, the number of children present and their ages, and the cleanliness of the place. I would watch for Dorica's reactions during and after a visit. Words she picked up or gestures she made could tell me a lot about her experience.

When Dorica seemed ready to remain there without me, I sent one of her favorite books along with her as a test. When she returned home, I read the book to her and observed her reactions: Would she smile at the pictures? Frown? Show fear? I could sense if she and the babysitter had played out certain parts of the book, or if the babysitter had not read it to her at all. Her reactions would tell me what she had experienced there. You might develop your own way of testing your child's experience away from home. Even a nonverbal child can tell you. Trust your feelings.

When choosing a babysitter, be sure to assess that person's skills and credentials. A teenager from the neighborhood will likely not possess the maturity and experience to take care of your child. We looked for staff members at Dorica's day care settings who wanted extra work. They were skilled and reliable, and we knew them personally. We sought people whose families were known to us. This gave us a broader sense of the person's reliability and character. We preferred candidates who could perform CPR if needed, and who had the capacity to coordinate with our nurse if something seemed amiss.

When entrusting your child to a babysitter, make sure you know where you child is at all times, and who else is around. Whenever a babysitter wanted to take Dorica to the movies, for instance, I insisted on knowing the movie, where it was being shown, at what time, and who would accompany them. Until I got to know the babysitter well, I would drop by to make sure they were where they said they would be. I might watch from the parking lot to observe their interactions as they came out of the movie. This may sound overprotective, but I learned that steps like these helped me safeguard Dorica. Don't be afraid to be vigilant.

Trust your intuition when your child is out of your sight. You can actually train yourself to pick up on subtle messages—almost a sixth sense—when your child is in trouble. If you sense something amiss, try to mentally send your child messages of support. Imagine that you are picking up your phone and saying to your child, "I'll be there in a few minutes. Hang in there." Special ones are very adept at picking up these signals. This will calm them, and they will relax until you arrive. Dorica and I developed this kind of telepathic connection in the days before cellular phones. It worked amazingly well.

Times have changed since we hired babysitters for Dorica. Many municipalities and states now have regulations about skills required for babysitting special needs children. Research your local laws. Ask your social worker for guidance and for recommendations for qualified babysitters. Social workers can provide excellent resources where this is concerned.

Along these lines, make sure to conduct a background check before hiring a babysitter. Special needs children are especially vulnerable to physical, emotional, and sexual abuse, since they often cannot communicate their experiences. You will want to know that the person you are hiring does not have a violent past or criminal record.

Taking Time Away

Most parents of special needs children fret over whether to take vacations or make trips without their child. I find that the biggest problem is not how children fare, but parents' own feelings of guilt. With a good, sensitive support system, coupled with knowing your babysitter's team, your child will be just fine when you are gone. In fact, he or she will pick up new skills, relish the freedom, and make new friends. You and your child both will benefit from breaks.

When I returned from trips away, I was amazed to learn about the new toys Dorica played with, the words she had picked up, the new songs she could sing, and the improvements she made with potty training. I never saw evidence that she had suffered. In fact, she would greet me with a smile from ear to ear upon my return. One time she taught me "La Cucaracha," which she learned while I was away. It became a staple in her repertoire of songs.

Brian and I did take a few vacations with Dorica. One time we drove south on Highway 1 along the California coast. We explored the ocean, built sandcastles, ate at many fast food joints, and had a fabulous time. Dorica rose to the occasion. We lined up the toys in the back seat, and Brian and I took turns entertaining her. She loved the attention.

We took her to Hawaii a couple of times. She loved the warm ocean water. We rented an apartment so we could cook and save on restaurant costs. Once we set a goal, we somehow managed to accomplish it. Vacations with her were important for us.

Still, it took Dorica a few days to adjust to the change in routine. At home, typically one of us would take her places. In that context, she knew how to ensure that she would remain the center of attention. On vacation, we went places together. When we weren't entertaining her, Brian and I talked to each other. This frustrated her strategy. She would try all kinds of little manipulations to win over our attention. We learned to present a united front. For instance, when he said "no" to more chocolate, I said it, too. Dorica learned to adjust.

Managing Behavioral Problems

With all of their delightful gifts, special needs children will invariably annoy you with behavioral problems, mostly at the wrong times. Dorica never had outright tantrums—somehow she knew how far she could go with a crying fit, biting her fingers, or some other nuisance. Early on I learned to check in with her when I saw her getting frustrated and upset to find out what was really bothering her. I felt like I needed to stay calm and not escalate the situation.

This is often easier said than done. For instance, one time I found Dorica making loud banging noises in the kitchen. I walked in to find that she had smeared ketchup all over the table. She wanted to mix mustard into the ketchup and spread it on bread to make a sandwich, but could not open the mustard bottle. In her frustration, she was banging it against the table. That was the noise I heard.

I could have taken away both containers and cleaned up the table, which would have frustrated her further, or I could have played along. I understood her need for self-determination in the situation—she felt she could make her own sandwich and that I should get out of the way. I needed to find a way to redirect her impulses into something more constructive.

So I calmly walked over to the counter, where I took out a sheet of aluminum foil. I opened the mustard bottle and got out a spoon. I spooned some mustard onto the bread, and invited her to do the same. She brought over the ketchup and made the sandwich herself. It became fun for her, like an experiment. When she tasted it, of course she found it not very appealing. She learned that this combination of condiments did not make for a very good snack. Then we addressed the underlying reason she made the sandwich in the first place. She was hungry.

I knew that saying "no" would backfire, and that it was important to honor Dorica's impulses. At times like these, it behooves parents of special needs children, especially those with autism, to discern the child's motivations and redirect their behaviors instead. Moments like these force us as parents to choose. We can react based on our expectations of how children should behave, or we can slow down, learn patience, tap into what our child needs or is trying to express, and live in the moment.

Most children want to please their parents. They do not want to act out and have tantrums. Outbursts are usually their last resort. Tantrums and other inappropriate behaviors often have triggers that might not be readily apparent. For autistic children, triggers can include loud noises, someone speaking too quickly, or using language too complex for them to comprehend. Sudden movements and negative comments by adults can trigger tantrums in special needs children as well. Part of our task as parents involves discovering what triggers our child so we can prevent the unwanted behaviors.

I remember one time when Dorica started waking up after only two hours of sleep. I could not figure it out. So I decided to investigate. I lay down in bed with her and realized that her new stereo had a blinking blue light, which was visible even when I closed my eyes. It was annoying. I unplugged the device, and the problem disappeared. Dorica slept through the night. From then on, I made sure to unplug the stereo each night before she went to bed.

I was lucky to discover the cause of this problem. It made me wonder how many other children face similar problems with electronics and have no way of telling us. We need to be vigilant about televisions, bed monitors, alarm clocks, and all kinds of flickering gadgets.

Nature and Routines

Special children are happiest when we let them tune into natural daily rhythms. In the morning, they typically wake up ready to embrace each new day, and in the evening they totally shut down to rejuvenate. They are much more connected to natural rhythms than we are.

I found that my daughter does best with routines. When she comes home on weekends now, she knows when it is time to greet the sun, eat breakfast, take a walk, cook, or take a nap. The more consistency, the happier she is. She has favorite toys and books, which never seem to grow old to her. She always seems to find something fun in them, or something new to learn about the world—even when I think it is time to throw them out.

B. Choosing the Right School Setting

When your child reaches school age, you will have to decide where to place him or her. This prompts the question that every parent with a special needs child must answer: How capable is my child, and how handicapped? Your pediatrician can help you answer this question and identify an appropriate school setting for your child.

In our case, we enrolled Dorica in a Montessori School for preschool, in the hopes that she would thrive in a more hands-on environment. We thought she would benefit from art lessons, and we planned to reinforce her school learning at home. While she thrived socially, however, she made very slow progress. Even after a half-year she was still drawing and painting circles, an indication of her very low level of development.

The teachers were wonderful and really tried their best. The school required that children be potty-trained, but it made an exception for Dorica. Given that the program lasted for just a few hours in the morning, the teachers did not have to change her diaper, so things worked out fine. Dorica made a loving, friendly addition to the school. She socialized well with others and liked to play with blocks, cars, and puzzles. But she would not work on her own. Somebody needed to sit next to her and motivate her.

The Montessori School was an excellent setting for her at that stage. She could not advance to a higher grade level, however, and she was becoming the tallest girl in the lowest grade.

After almost one and a half years, we knew it was time to find her another school.

For autistic children or children with attention deficit hyperactivity disorder (ADHD), I would suggest starting out with a Montessori School. It confers several advantages: it has a very low teacher/student ratio; it focuses on art and hands-on learning; it encourages solving behavior problems through verbalization; and it teaches socialization skills.

After a year we started looking into programs specifically geared toward the developmentally delayed. In our county (Contra Costa), we found a day care center that provides services and schooling for people with disabilities from childhood through adulthood. Many counties have these adult care centers. Ours is called the Community Access Program (CAP) – Hilltop Care Center. In order to qualify, Dorica had to become a client of the Regional Center of the East Bay (RCEB), which funds CAP – Hilltop. I highly recommend CAP – Hilltop and programs like it. Many other programs stop at age eighteen or twenty-five, and it can be difficult to find other settings for those ages. (See "Transitioning to Adult Services" later in this chapter.)

My daughter knows the Center and loves its teachers and caregivers. It is a safe, caring environment. The program runs five days a week from 9:00 a.m. to 2:00 p.m. A bus picks up Dorica in the morning and brings her back in the afternoon. I can call whenever I have a question, and I can visit any time. I feel welcomed and supported.

The CAP – Hilltop program assigned Dorica a social worker, who has remained with us throughout the years. The social worker checks in with Dorica every three months and conducts the annual review of her individual service plan. This review engages parents, care workers, social workers, and others. It includes a comprehensive assessment of the skills Dorica has mastered and establishes goals for her further development.

The social worker has been a critical support for us since the beginning. During Dorica's school-age years, the social worker connected Dorica with different school settings, including integrating her into regular classrooms and work centers. We always came back to Hilltop, as it has proven to be the best choice for her.

Finding the right care setting for a developmentally delayed child is so important. It gives our special ones a place to work, shine, and socialize, and it enables working parents to pursue their professional lives. We need to accept that our children cannot be around us twenty-four hours a day. They need to feel appreciated by their peers and build friendships and self-esteem. It is important for them to learn and strive for independence to whatever extent they can achieve it.

C. Navigating in the Community

Being Out in Public

All parents of special needs children will have to come to terms with reactions from other people. These can range from curiosity to judgment to outright hostility. Staring will happen often. The fact is, most people don't understand much about special needs children.

Throughout the years people have asked why Dorica has intellectual disabilities and whether we had considered genetic testing. Of course, Brian and I had asked ourselves these questions as well, but it always seemed jarring coming from others. We received our share of prejudice and judgment.

When Dorica was very young and we were still living in Germany, I sometimes kept her home because I did not want to face the stares and judgments. The environment was different there than it was in the United States. Germany had many thousands of special needs children, yet, those children were not well-integrated into society. They rarely left their family's houses.

Sometimes when I took Dorica out as a young child and she did not respond when other parents spoke to her, I would make up an excuse that it was not her day. Some days I simply did not have the energy to explain Dorica's condition to strangers.

Parents should not feel compelled to divulge every detail about their child to every curious seeker.

As time went on, people's reactions actually got easier to deal with. I came to understand that people are genuinely curious, and they do not always know how to communicate their curiosity tactfully. How we answer questions can either inform or fuel more prejudice. A lot depends on how we see our role and answer our calling.

Eventually, I stopped caring what people said or thought. I began to see bringing Dorica out in public as a way to teach others. To minimize negative reactions, I still always make sure to dress Dorica appropriately when we go out.

Beyond that, I let Dorica work her magic: Between Dorica's joyful spirit and complete lack of self-consciousness, she ends up inviting everyone around her to lighten up, lose their inhibitions, and smile. When children see Dorica touching and hugging a tree, they begin touching and hugging trees too. When we go to Costco, Dorica likes to stand in the parking lot and wave to trucks as they come and go. Before long, truck drivers are laughing, smiling, and waving back. We do the same in the park, which has a railroad overpass. From above we see passengers waving and smiling in response to Dorica. Her infectious enthusiasm transforms the environment wherever we go.

Special needs children teach people different ways of doing things. They help us break down barriers. Taking them out in public allows them to fill this important social function. From this perspective, bringing special needs children out in public becomes an exercise in teaching and benefiting everyone who comes in contact with them.

I would advise you not to let fear of others' reactions stop you. Do not let people's superficial judgments make you retreat and become invisible. In fact, you almost owe it to your child to be proactive, and to use those awkward encounters as teachable moments. You have just as much right to be here on this earth, as does your child. Being a parent of a special needs child is a mission. Stand tall in your role, and find compassion for those who do not yet understand.

Allow Your Child to Help You Build Community

I am always surprised by how many people feel touched by Dorica's smile, or who start smiling at her. People might come forward to help, but the line blurs between who is helping whom! Dorica raises the vibration wherever we go. Everyone benefits.

If you belong to a church and find it calming and soothing for your soul, take your child along. Allow your child to sing and dance there. Regular attendance gives people a chance to know you and your child. It creates a sense of community that can benefit your child—and you too. You might find an elderly person who is looking for companionship and even offers babysitting. Other members might suggest resources that you are not familiar with. Think about the possibilities and start networking.

There are other ways to build community as well, where you can share your joys and struggles. Our neighborhood is a good example. One neighbor is an excellent cook and comes by with a dish for Dorica now and then. I express my gratitude by offering to watch her place when she and her husband go away on vacation. Get out there and let your sunshine touch the souls of the people around you.

Our neighborhood has people from many different cultures, each of whom connects with Dorica in unique and positive ways. A Chinese neighbor brings beautiful floral bouquets over and just likes to say "hello" to Dorica. Another, from El Salvador, invites us over for incredibly delicious barbecues. An African-American neighbor plays old Elvis Presley and other rock albums on vinyl for Dorica. He teaches her dance moves, and they dance together. They share an unspoken language and a special bond.

We have built a strong, supportive community where I live. Again, the question often is, who is supporting whom? Little children hear about Dorica and ride their bikes over to meet her. They even dare play ball with her—with big, old beach balls. Once a year I invite the neighborhood to my back yard, where we gather around the fireplace. On July 4, a neighbor invites us over to light forbidden rockets and fireworks. The parents and children have tons of fun. People have birthdays and invite Dorica and me for the parties. Someone dies, and we attend the funeral. The neighborhood changes, but Dorica has remained part of it all. She has never been shy. She goes up to all the neighbors and says "hi." That pure goodness of hers is irresistible. She has helped us create a strong community.

Give your special one the chance to create community around you. You may be surprised at how much everyone benefits.

Connect with Other Parents

Extend your network to other parents of special ones. Parents really want to connect with and help each other. We found it very easy to make friends with parents through Dorica's day care center and schooling. We shared information, gave each other support and strength, and laughed and joked together. We sometimes even went places with our children in tow.

For instance, I know a father whose child has cerebral palsy and is in a wheelchair. He always brings his son to the farmer's market in El Cerrito. Seeing each other and saying "hello" is part of the routine. This father is so supportive and positive, he can light up the whole farmer's market. He is a true inspiration. We wheel our children along and collect free apples and fruit samples, teaching by example. Dorica and her buddy like to visit the man who plays guitar, and they rock up a storm. People around us begin to smile—they cannot help it. They stop and congratulate us. Nothing else needs to be done. Our special ones spread happiness wherever they go.

Consider arranging outings with other parents and their children. These can be a lot of fun and a huge source of moral support. Try something new. We've gone with other parents and their children to yoga classes, on train rides through the woods, and to swimming pools. We have used these opportunities to bring the outside world to our children while building community. Through a sense of common purpose, we have made an incredible difference for our children and each other.

Follow Your Child's Interests

Find activities that engage your child's interests and natural curiosity. Don't be afraid to take a risk. Your child might surprise you with what he or she is willing to try or learn. We can forget that special needs children can be just as adventurous as typical children, though they may show it in different ways.

For instance, one time I took Dorica to a park that features several old railroad cars. Visitors can climb ladders up to the top of the cars for a better view. At first the ladders scared Dorica. She would not climb them no matter how much I coaxed her.

A few days later, I heard her making sounds of a train. I got out books and we looked at pictures of trains and even blew a train whistle. I knew she was telling me she wanted to go back and climb the trains. So I brought her back. Once there, she mustered up the courage to climb two stairs. That was it. It was a start. We went home.

The next time she climbed four stairs. After a few more visits and attempts at climbing, her curiosity finally won out. She climbed up to the top—eight stairs in all. Her beaming, smiling face said it all—she did the impossible. We stomped on the old train, got greasy and dirty, and who knows how we got down the ladder.

If your child wants to try something new, indulge him or her. If he or she shies away from something, your child may just need some gentle encouragement. Be patient with the process. It will be worth the effort.

Because Dorica loves people so much, she found her own ways to get out into the community. Through her day care center, Dorica visited senior centers and nursing homes as part of the Meals on Wheels program. She made many friends doing this and became the darling of the program. She would take time and sit with the bedridden seniors, holding their hands, stroking their arms, and giving out hugs. She made them feel happy and spread joy and peace.

While Dorica loves people, she feels ambivalent about animals. Many special needs children, however, feel an immediate, strong bond with animals. The nonverbal nature of the relationship allows them to connect in profound, delightful ways. Special needs children tend to possess an intrinsic understanding and appreciation for animals.

If you don't have a companion animal at home, search for animal-assisted therapy programs in your area. These might involve dogs, cats, or even horses. I know the Oakland Zoo had a program where they allowed special needs children to feed the animals. Organizations such as the Delta Society and The Good Dog Foundation in the New York area provide therapy dogs services.

Exercise and Fun

Be sure to give your child opportunities to get exercise. Special needs children need to move their bodies just as much as typical children do. Dorica takes an exercise class every day at the day care center. When she comes home, we do even more. Every weekend we go for about a two-hour stroll through the park. She exercises with my *Easy Yoga by Peggy* DVD. She has a stationary bike and a rowing machine. She loves everything that gets her moving. We go to playgrounds and she uses the swings, the slides, and the bars for stretching. We also like to go to Calistoga for the mineral pools.

The main criteria I have for any activity we choose is whether Dorica has fun and enjoys it. Fortunately, she sees just about everything in life as fun. This is very common among special needs children. Allow their sense of fun and adventure to enrich your life and the lives of people in your community.

D. Transitioning to Adult Services

One of the first realities that hits parents upon learning of their child's special needs is that he or she will likely require a lifetime of care. Because development and needs can vary so much depending on the child's condition, navigating transitions from one care setting to another—and knowing when to change settings—can be challenging. This becomes even trickier when a special needs child ages out of school, which typically happens between the ages of eighteen and twenty-six.

In her book, *Facing Learning Disabilities in the Adult Years*, Joan Shapiro reminds us that we need to consider the needs of adults with disabilities as distinctly different from those of children with disabilities. She writes about learning disabilities, but her approach applies just as well to people with developmental disabilities:

> "Learning disabilities are expressed differently at different ages and stages in life. The impact of the disability on an adult is influenced by changing educational, social, personal, and occupational demands. Adults with learning disabilities cannot be regarded as children with learning disabilities grown up. Instead, adults with learning disabilities are a distinct group with unique characteristics and needs."

I was very fortunate to have had a team of experts guide me through the transitional phases with Dorica. They helped me understand Dorica's needs at each stage, and they steered us through the maze of services and application processes. Importantly, they prepared me with potential scenarios I could expect in the future.

For instance, when Dorica was eighteen years old, my team suggested that she could eventually qualify for a job placement, which would be coordinated through the adult day care center. Joan Shapiro points out in her book that this kind of advance transition planning has become standard practice. Educators begin screening special needs children for career skills and competencies as early as elementary school, and these assessments continue through high school. Tutoring and small group instruction has become the norm in an effort to integrate special needs children into the workplace.

The staff at Dorica's day care center assessed her skills and saw that she could learn how to wash dishes. They taught her how to bring dishes to the sink, wash them, and place them on the racks. That prepared her for the job placement at Popeye's. Despite their best efforts, Dorica did not last very long. One of the reasons was that she could not stand for a long time and got lightheaded. At that point she would lie down on the floor for a few minutes, then get up and continue. But in a restaurant setting this is not feasible. There might have been other workshop place choices, but it was not easy to find a different work setting without a long commute or a work she could do.

So what happens when a special needs child ages out of school and cannot find or succeed in a job placement? Moments like this can create incredible challenges for parents, as programs for adults with special needs often have lengthy waiting lists. Your child could end up back home for two years—a common waiting period for finding a placement for adult services.

Here are some suggestions based on my own experience to help you navigate transitions to adult services.

Plan ahead. Work with your care team well in advance of your child's needs. A good rule of thumb is to plan two years ahead. Where will you want your child to live and receive care? Attend open houses for care facilities. Register for special trips organized by your current disability center. Talk to clients in those facilities to get a feel for the setting. What is the tone? What activities do they provide? Who are the aides? What food do they serve? How clean are the rooms and the kitchens? And finally, get on the waiting lists.

Prepare your child for a life away from home. As I have discussed, your special needs child will develop unique ways of coping and will often exhibit personality traits you never thought possible. Recognize that your child may have strengths and interests that he or she does not show you. Listen to what teachers and other caretakers have to say about your child when you are not around. These observations will give you clues about your child's ability to navigate life away from home. We spend so much time with our special needs children that we can easily forget they have other sides and capacities.

As your child grows older, he or she will spend more time away from home, and others will provide a greater share of care. The more your child leaves home, the more he or she will draw on the strength and coping skills you imparted. There may come a time when you realize your child needs to live apart from you.

For me, that time came unexpectedly, but in retrospect, at the perfect moment. Dorica was thirty-eight years old. She was healthy, and we were both content. One of my reliable babysitters moved away, and I needed to find a backup. This prompted me to search for other options. Dorica's social worker helped me find a board-and-care home for her, where she could stay overnight and still attend the CAP – Hilltop Care Center.

Initially, I explored the home only as a possibility. But it began to occur to me: Maybe she was ready to face the world without me hovering over her. She had learned enough coping skills to weather life. She was young enough to build new friendships and learn new things. It was the right time to make the change. I trusted the process.

Sure enough, after a few challenging weeks, she adjusted beautifully. She began to talk more, and she let her caretakers know what she wanted—like cookies in the middle of the night. The staff at the board-and-care home played with her, sang with her, read books to her, and did Zumba exercises with her. I could never do all these activities at home with her. She gained peers, who became her friends, and who she learned from. She became the sweetheart of the whole home—for aides, caretakers, and residents alike.

We developed a routine where Terra or I pick her up on the weekends, and she stays at the board-and-care home during the week. She loves to come home and show me what she has learned. I love to have her at home and go to places we have visited before. After a weekend of soaking up love we are both ready to face the world again. I am confident that when I am not around anymore she will have helpers, a caseworker who cares, and Terra, her half-sister and biggest fan. Again, I am trusting the process.

As Dorica and I have both gotten older, my task has become playing more of a supportive role in the background so that she feels we are working together as a team. Life has become easier for me now. I like to help the staff at the Hilltop Care Center and the board-and-care home by providing lunches, food, or whatever else they need. We all have a good rapport, and I feel confident that Dorica is in a safe and caring environment.

As you explore possibilities for placing your adult child with special needs, consider visiting nursing homes and board-and-care homes at levels 1, 2, 3, and 4. (Higher numbers indicate more needed care.) If your child has fewer needs and greater function, you may wish to explore independent living arrangements. Service agencies can provide training to help special needs adults to live independently without supervision and support services.

Your social worker can make recommendations and connect you with facilities that match even limited budgets. Trust your inner guidance and gut feelings when making these decisions.

E. Planning for the Future

Whenever someone asked how long Dorica could live, Brian always responded, "Dorica lives forever." There's some truth to that—she's still going strong after all these years. In all likelihood, Dorica will outlive me.

Most parents with special needs children will need to plan for the time when they are no longer around to care for their children. While certain conditions shorten the lives of special needs children, the fact is that most conditions are not life-threatening.

Our social worker helped me plan for the future. She connected me with a lawyer who set up a Special Needs Trust, which specifies my last wishes and identifies who will care for Dorica when I am gone. The lawyer helped me draw up advance medical directives should I become incapacitated. With our social worker's help, I made my own funeral arrangements. Social workers can provide a font of resources here. They can connect you with lawyers, classes, and other services to help you attend to your last wishes.

These tasks may not be enjoyable, but completing them will give you the comfort of knowing that you have done your best to care for your child. In doing so, you will clarify your wishes and make things easier for the caretakers you leave behind.

A Reason for Special Needs Children

With all the unique challenges that special needs children present, and with all the accommodations and adaptations that parents need to make as a result, I believe these children come into our lives for a reason.

Consider the case of Brooke Greenberg. Born in 1993, she never grew beyond the size of a toddler, and she remained cognitively at the level of a two-year-old. Mysteriously, she stopped aging when she was five years old. Her doctors termed her condition Syndrome X. At her death in 2013, she became widely known as the "twenty-year-old toddler."

But what of her life?

Doctors and scientists became fascinated with her mysterious condition and studied her DNA. They wondered whether its mutations could hold secrets to slowing the human aging process or curing other diseases. Could this girl who stopped aging reduce the burden of disease and improve human well-being?

Certainly, Brooke contributed to the well-being of the people around her. One of four girls, Brooke brought incredible joy to her family and was showered with love and affection. Her sisters and parents cherished her. She loved to be cuddled and tickled.

Her parents reported that she developed a strong identity and a rebellious streak. When her younger sister, Carly, was born, she became jealous, like any other child would be. And despite the challenges the family faced over the years, their devotion never wavered.

Her mother, Melanie Greenberg said, "The older she gets, it's unbelievable…. everybody just wants to hold her." Her father called her "his angel."[6]

Like so many special needs children, Brooke expressed and inspired unconditional love. This is the magic our special ones make and the gifts they give to humanity.

Chapter 6

PRACTICAL SUGGESTIONS FOR TEACHERS AND OTHER EDUCATORS WHO SERVE SPECIAL NEEDS CHILDREN

> *"What would happen...if they simply went on assuming their children would do everything? Perhaps not quickly. Perhaps not by the book. But what if they simply erased those growth and development charts, with their precise, constricting points and curves? What if they kept their expectations but erased the time line? What harm could it do? Why not try?"*
> —*Kim Edwards,* The Memory Keeper's Daughter

This chapter provides insights, tips, and tools for professionals who work with special needs children. The first half focuses on teachers. The second half addresses educators outside the classroom—principals, administrators, supervisors, coaches, and testing coordinators.

Here, I draw from my twenty-five years of experience as an elementary school teacher in the Oakland public schools, a large inner city school system. The campus where I taught had multiple grade levels and special education classes. I learned first-hand what worked with special needs students in the classroom, and what did not.

Over the years, education goals and philosophies evolved. Special education went from being a separate program to being integrated into the regular classroom. To accommodate this shift, teachers received special training and some extra support.

It was both challenging and rewarding. I had about thirty regular students and two to three special education students each year. I had no classroom aide. Teachers in our school system only got an aide when a physically challenged student in a wheelchair needed help—and even then it was for physical, not educational support.

I earned my master's degree in education from the University of California, Berkeley. Throughout the years I followed new paradigms and directions in teaching children with learning disabilities. I experienced first-hand the problems and burdens that standardized testing mandated by "No Child Left Behind" created for teachers and students.

With all the requirements placed on teachers today, attending to special needs children can be very challenging. I hope that these techniques, which I used in my classroom, can ease some of those challenges and help you discover the reward of working with special needs students.

Suggestions for Teachers

Suggestion #1: Read the IEP. Most of the time, regular (non-special education) teachers get assigned one or more students who have a learning disability or who have special needs and a physical disability. The student's Individualized Education Plan (IEP) serves as a critical guide to help teachers address the specific learning needs of a special needs child. It summarizes a child's test scores and educational needs. Developed with parents, it also sets learning goals for the child and identifies services the school will provide.

As a teacher, you already have too much to do. Still, take the time to read the IEP. It will save you time in the long run. The IEP reads like a story and timeline of the youngster's life. It provides insights into significant events and their impact such as bedwetting, tantrums, social withdrawal, being verbally aggressive, and so on. It includes test scores, an educational history, and goals that you will be held responsible to help meet. It will help you understand the child and more quickly adjust your teaching style to meet his or her needs.

Suggestion #2: Invite Parents to Chat. Parents of special needs children can become your greatest allies when you invite them to become active partners. Invite parents to the school to chat with you, and ask them about their home life with their child. What are the highs and lows? What challenges do they face? What do parents and their child enjoy doing together? With this in mind, consider the child's learning goals and identify simple steps parents can take to help reach them.

For instance, perhaps telling time has been identified as one learning goal. To help meet it, encourage teeth brushing at 7:00 p.m. each night. Not only will the child learn to tell time, he or she will learn about responsibility and health. It can become a fun, special time for the parent and child. Work with parents to develop creative, easy ways to reinforce school-day learning.

Suggestion #3: Send a "Happy Face" Sticker Home on a Folder Daily. The sticker could be for a goal you and a parent set for the child, like good behavior or completed homework and/or classwork. Add a sticker to the folder, that could contain homework, classwork, assignments, schedules, behavior chart, every day. It is a simple yet powerful way to communicate with the parent about a job well done. It reinforces the agreements you made and builds a parent's and child's self-esteem. The parent knows that you care. (If you stop sending stickers home, parents will visit your classroom and ask why!)

Suggestion #4: Invite Parents to Your Classroom as a Special Treat. This could be for the performance of a play, a recital of a poem for Martin Luther King Day or other special day, or an award ceremony to recognize who has turned in the most homework. The invitation should be to acknowledge something that the special needs child has mastered or worked hard for along with the rest of the class. Inviting the parent makes the child and parent feel proud. Parents love it.

Suggestion #5: Ask the Student Three Open-Ended Questions During the Day. Asking open-ended questions of students demonstrates your interest in them, and it motivates them to keep striving. It absolutely lights children up. One day, I began by asking a student a question related to his home life: "What did your new puppy do yesterday?" Later in the day I asked him a question that related positively to school: "How did you get the protractor moving to make such a fine circle?" Then I asked him a question that he would take home after school: "After you get home, what would you like to do with the puppy picture that you drew today?" Use this kind of model (questions relating to home, school, and after-school) to deepen your relationships with special needs children and motivate them to learn.

Suggestion #6: Keep Routines Going. Most children do best in a classroom that has predictable routines. They provide a framework for children to function and become successful. For children with attention deficit disorder (ADD), attention deficit hyperactivity disorder (ADHD), learning disabilities (LD), and Asperger syndrome, certain routines help them make sense of challenging situations.

A routine might be as simple as having a coat rack with the name of each student above a hook instead of letting students randomly choose hooks to hang their coats on. Predictable routines create a more orderly atmosphere. The simple action of hanging one's coat in a prescribed place first thing in the morning sets the tone for the day.

Another way I created routines was to follow the same format with lessons. With math, for instance, I would have students focus first on the new lesson from the book, then proceed to independent practice, where they worked on workbook pages. This predictable routine helped all students master the materials, which they could then review at home.

When we needed to walk somewhere, we practiced a procedure where children would line up in single file and place their right hands on the back of the person in front of them. It took almost a week at the beginning of the year for the children to learn it, but then they would quickly line up when needed. This routine works wonders in emergencies and lock-downs.

Students also like consistent homework procedures. For math, reading, and writing, I would assign two to three pages a day, four days a week. Students knew exactly what they needed to do, and when they needed to do it. It took the chaos out of the equation.

Suggestion #7: Let Students Teach and Help Each Other. A buddy system for special needs students is almost a must. Assign bathroom-break buddies, coaching and tutoring buddies, buddies for running errands, play buddies, cafeteria buddies, and so on. Most of the students love to have jobs to help out. They take their roles very seriously in most cases. It increases classroom engagement and builds rapport among students.

Suggestion #8: Create a Friendly and Positive Learning Environment. All students want to be loved and accepted. They want to feel that their teacher cares. One easy and simple way to do this is to hang students' completed work on the classroom walls. Students beam with pride when they see their work displayed. When you show them you care, they start caring too.

An expression of caring can help redirect unwanted child behaviors. Once, I had a special education student who needed to crumple up twenty pages of paper before he could settle into a task. The area around his desk looked very messy. I made it a point to clean it up periodically during the day. He finally understood that I cared enough and after a few weeks stopped the behavior on his own. He became our "Mr. Neat," encouraging others to pick up after themselves.

It was always important to me that the classroom be neat and clean when students arrived in the morning, regardless of whether a custodian had made the rounds or not. If it took me forty-five minutes to sweep the floor, order the books on the shelves, and line up the desks, so be it. I made sure that when students entered the classroom we started on time—without wasting precious teaching minutes.

Colors and color-coding worked wonders for creating order and predictability. I used green folders for homework, blue for "work in progress," and so on. The students knew what each color meant. I required that students bring six sharpened pencils with them each morning so that we wasted no class time looking for something to write with. Special education students especially need a quiet, focused work routine. As a teacher I had to plan ahead to eliminate chaos and distractions.

Suggestion #9: Be Friendly and Positive Toward Students and Teachers. Typical students pick up very quickly whether you support a special education student or not. They listen to your voice, study the looks you give, and scan your mannerisms. They are very sensitive to injustice, harshness, yelling, and other negativity. I found that, in most cases classmates want the best for the student who has a disability.

Students will help, tutor, and show respect for special needs children, and they want the same from their teachers. It is up to you to set the tone for a positive learning environment by being friendly and supportive to everyone—students and other teachers. Students often hear teachers talking to each other, and they absorb negative remarks unconsciously.

Teachers can reverse negative behaviors among even the most disruptive students by being friendly and positive, and by praising students. One year, for instance, another teacher and I knew we were about to each get such a student in each of our classes. We learned about the negative reputations of these two students from their previous teachers.

Sure enough, just days after the year began, these students started to challenge us. They would just leave the classroom or even start fires under their desk. They sprayed ketchup in other students' hair. Anything was possible.

Instead of sending them to the office we invited them to eat lunch with us. We bought a garden table, chairs, and umbrella and set up our teacher's picnic area. We both had the same lunchtime, which worked out well. This was something new for our "villains", as they were known to get into daily fights on the yard during lunch. We hatched our plan: When one of them sat with us, we talked "teacher talk" about the other child—but in the most positive way. We might say, "Wow, did you see the lion he drew? You have to see it." And so on. The one sitting around us—eating the special cookies we had brought for them—heard us make our glowing remarks.

Then we worked on the other child the same way. If they were both with us we found something positive to say about each of them. We showed off their good work to other teachers. The mere act of saying something positive about them got those children coming back to our lunch table each day. Soon other students wanted to join us, and we praised the "problem kids" in front of them. The whole dynamic changed. All of a sudden they wanted to be the stars.

In just two months, having spent twenty to twenty-five minutes with them each day, we reversed their negative behaviors. We had no major problems from either of them for the rest of the year. We didn't even need to continue with our picnic table. My fellow teacher and I worked as a team on behalf of our little customers, as we called them.

By being friendly and positive we can improve the lives of students, even those with difficult behavioral patterns. Praise can lift the self-esteem of any student. Challenged students often need it the most.

Suggestion #10: Pair with another Teacher as a Support Buddy. The example I just recounted about the "villains" showed how effectively teachers can support each other. When I was a teacher, I never knew which students would enter my classroom, nor what their needs would be. The administration assigned students to me based on many criteria. I often found that I needed another teacher as a support buddy to share tips and problem-solving strategies, such as the lunchtime compliments we gave those "problem children" so I could effectively work with the more challenging students.

I paired with teachers who taught next door or at the same grade level. We brainstormed and established agreements about how we would handle special needs children. Students came to understand that they would be treated the same way whether they were in my classroom or that of my fellow teacher.

My buddy and I became a team. We helped each other out. When a student acted out or had a meltdown in my class, I could send him or her to my teacher-buddy's classroom to calm down, and vice versa. Sometimes we teamed up special needs students from each of our classes for part of the day. It worked wonders. By collaborating, we could provide better support for our students, and it took some of the pressure off each of us.

Suggestion #11: Stay Up-to-Date with IEPs, Required Paperwork, and Parent Meetings. When you have special education students in your classroom, you will be required by many agencies to prove that these students are learning and meeting established goals. The IEP provides a useful framework for you as a teacher, for the student, and for parents. Don't set the IEP aside. Use it as a living document to guide your teaching activities. Stay up-to-date on your paperwork so it does not pile up. You will be better prepared for required reporting.

Parents expect that you will work extensively with their child, and that you will hold regular meetings with everyone involved in that child's education. Keep these meetings positive. Parents like to see that a teacher takes a special interest in their child. Have students' progress reports on hand and be prepared to discuss them.

A great way to demonstrate your interest in students is to post pictures on the classroom walls featuring their work, and even pictures of the children themselves engaged in learning. Create a board where you display good test scores. Exhibit students' projects on a table in the classroom.

Students and parents love it when teachers point out and praise a student's work or project. It's even more effective when a teacher invites a student to explain the project. These kinds of visuals reinforce students' belief in themselves and their capacity to learn.

Suggestions for Educators Outside of the Classroom

Special needs children need support from a whole network of professionals, in addition to teachers. This section provides practical suggestions for the other educators who make up a special needs student's team.

I bring to this subject the unique perspective that I gained from going through training and coursework to become a principal. Through this education, I learned about the responsibilities of the entire team and what goes into placing children with disabilities.

My goal in becoming a principal was to support teachers and become an ally for students. I did not wish to remove myself from the classroom and become a distant figure walking the hallways and disappearing into an office. I wanted to become the kind of principal that students can talk to, feel supported by, and even laugh and have fun with. I hoped to make a positive difference for teachers and disenchanted students.

I completed two years of required study at California State University, Hayward, which qualified me to apply for the position of vice principal. When I learned more about the actual requirements of the job, however, I decided not to pursue it. I made this decision for two reasons.

First, I would have to spend most of my time disciplining students. That did not align with my values or the approach I felt would work best. Second, I would have to spend most evenings in meetings and around the school. I had to think about my own special needs daughter who needed her mother at night.

I decided that I had a better chance to make a difference in students' lives as a good, solid, and respected teacher. Still, the training gave me an outstanding education about what goes on behind the scenes in the field of education.

With this said, here are some suggestions for how other educators can support teachers who have challenging students or special needs children in the classroom.

Suggestion #1: Find Additional Resources and Therapies for Teachers. These could be materials such as games, toys, and hands-on manipulatives that teachers can use to supplement a lesson in class or send home with a learning-disabled student. Principals often know where these additional resources are located in the school or even at other schools. School budgets often allow for Title 1 additional allocated funding, which can be used to buy such helpful materials.

I remember one time when I needed a CD player for my classroom. My principal found one, and together we ordered classical music CDs to play during math lessons. This calmed students down and helped them score higher on tests. Special education students enjoyed music with everything, including math. I knew this from my own daughter.

Educators and coaches often know about therapies that have become available for use in the classroom. Special speech therapy sessions with a trained language specialist or music lessons with a music coach can help all students. My special education students loved to play the drums, bells, and rattles. A music teacher can teach a whole class how to play instruments, sing songs, or play a rhyme language game. Principals usually know how to find and hire these additional coaches—and locate the funding to pay for them.

I remember from my own classroom experience how much special education students enjoyed music and choir lessons. Their whole bodies relaxed and it was so much fun. Parents and teachers can request that special therapies be included in an IEP.

Another way of getting all students to move, relax, and enjoy life is by letting them dance as often as you can work it into your lesson plan. In my classroom we memorized timetables by dancing and singing them. It was hilarious. We all learned dances for Cinco de Mayo festivals, which created opportunities for inclusion and participation by all the students. Special needs students especially love dancing, singing, and performing.

Suggestion #2: Bring Volunteers into the Classroom. Volunteers can be wonderful resources. Special needs children need a lot of one-to-one time to learn tasks, and teachers have so little time to devote to that. Volunteers can read to the special needs students, teach them to place blocks in different slots, play games with them, help with classroom lessons, and accompany the students to the bathroom. These can really can help a teacher out. Grandmothers, mothers, retired teachers, and educators are all fair game. Principals often know where to find these wonderful volunteers.

Volunteers can be recruited during bake sales, fashion shows, student performances, and parent-teacher association (PTA) meetings. I remember one volunteer mother who taught my whole class how to cook soup. Everyone cut the vegetables and became part of preparing something healthy and nourishing. Another volunteer taught my class to paint totem poles. Hands-on activities are especially important for special education students.

Another time volunteers taught my class how to set up worm boxes for composting. It was amazing to see how much my special education students enjoyed it; they did not mind touching worms and soil at all. As a teacher I spent many weeks during summer vacations organizing field trips for my class, and finding as many willing volunteers to visit us and lead activities for my students.

For instance, a team of presenters from the Lawrence Hall of Science at Berkeley taught my class about dry ice and the universe, magnetism and electricity, and hydroponics. Wildlife refuge centers brought special animals to the classroom. The 4-H Club even brought cows and chickens to the school. Through that experience we raised chicks. My special education students enjoyed taking them home on weekends.

Suggestion #3: Work as a Team. Principals, coaches, and supervisors all play an important role in the lives of special education students. As a teacher I was fortunate to have had a principal whom I could depend on in case of a crisis. He knew that if I sent a student to him, it was serious. He could deflect a violent situation, call the parent, administer medication, monitor a seizure, and give the child time to express his or her frustration, anger, or fear, which was mostly the problem to begin with.

He would keep a student as long as necessary to calm him or her down and understand that we all cared. When I saw the principal walking back to my classroom with his arm over the student's shoulder I knew the problem was solved. I felt really appreciated when the student could give me a big hug when entering the classroom.

The same principal was also very good with special education students. He knew them all by name and gave them jobs to do outside their classroom routine. For instance, he assigned one to collect attendance sheets every day from each classroom. He had another fill bags with fruits and vegetables for parents of indigent students to take home. He had another accompany him in the car to run errands. These are just a few of the tasks he assigned to them. The special education students all felt important and took their jobs very seriously. It was interesting because by having the students around him, the principal heard first-hand what the teachers were doing or teaching in the classrooms.

When I went through the program to become a principal I realized that it would be much more important in the role that I offer students a shoulder to lean on rather than display toughness. This is especially true for special education students. They need a box of tissues and a place to vent frustrations, not handcuffs.

A principal's office can be a frightening place for students and teachers alike, but it need not be. It should be more a place to learn about new approaches or receive validation. It should be a safe place for teachers to voice their observations and develop mutually acceptable solutions.

Principals are in the unique position to see the big picture, and this can prove very beneficial. The principal often serves as the mediator between parents and teachers when problems develop. The more the principal knows about the student, the better he or she can engage parents to become part of the solution.

In my experience, the principals who were most effective were those who made themselves visible and available. Students were not afraid to drop into these principals' offices and ask for a ball or make a phone call. I admired the principal who would come into my classroom to share a funny story or invite us to play a game of baseball. These principals would give awards such as "Teacher of the Month," "Student of the Month," and even "Class of the Month." This kind of praise went a long way.

The principal is an important member of a special needs child's team. Other members of the team can include counselors, coaches, testing personnel from outside agencies, and so on. Each professional plays different and equally important roles in supporting that child. They can all help make a child's transitions easier by finding the right placements, therapies, teachers, and settings.

It is critical to remember that each member of this team may see a different side of the child. Think about it: As adults, we can switch from being a loving parent at home to being a disciplined and controlled executive in our work environment. Children do that too, no matter how disabled they are.

Sometimes it can be difficult to believe, but the child we think we know well may actually act differently with another professional or in another setting. It is important to keep this in mind, because different members of the child's team may have a perspective that can help others resolve challenges with that child. This is why it is so important to take a team approach with a special needs child.

Even I, a special needs teacher and mother of a special needs daughter, had to learn this lesson. Teachers, coaches, and aides would often surprise me with stories about how differently Dorica acted in school.

For instance, at home Dorica did not like it when I put cream, like sunscreen or moisturizer, on her face. She would tolerate it, but she would give me a look that told me how she really felt. It therefore came as a complete surprise when I saw photos her teacher had taken of Dorica wearing makeup and lipstick. How on Earth did she get my daughter to do this when I had such a hard time of it? And how did she get Dorica to smile? I spoke with the teacher about it.

Apparently, the teacher staged photo shoots in class. Dorica got applause, hugs, and kisses from all the students as the teacher made her up for the shoot. Then I understood: Dorica did it because she loves to be the center of attention. And it even went further. Several times a day she would pull out the makeup kit and drag any warm body to help her with the mirror, apply the makeup, and do her hair. It was hilarious. Her teacher and I had a good laugh together.

I never let on to Dorica that I knew about this. A daughter is entitled to some secrets, and a mother does not need to know everything. Still, I never would have known about this behavior had the teacher not shown me Dorica's photographs.

I experienced the other side of this phenomenon as a teacher in my own classroom. I remember one special education student whose mother approached me about the difficulty her child was having with his math homework. Apparently, her son would often refuse to complete the simple addition assignments I gave him. If he actually did the assignments, it would take him until almost midnight to finish—and only with his mother's help.

The mother complained that the work was too hard, took too long, and accomplished nothing. She even went to the principal and asked for her child to be excused from this torture and any type of homework. (Does this sound familiar to readers who are teachers?)

Yet in class, this child routinely completed these kinds of assignments without any problem. The parent could not believe what I was telling her, so I set up a scenario where she could hear and experience it for herself.

I was fortunate to have a teaching buddy in the classroom next door, which was separated by a door. We discussed our plan with the principal: My teaching buddy would have his students leave the classroom, and this parent and the principal would slip in through an outside door. I would leave the door separating the two classrooms ajar and hold my regular lesson.

It worked like a charm. My special education student had no clue what we were up to. I gave the lesson as I normally did, and I handed out the practice sheet. The students had fifteen minutes to complete the assignment. At the end of fifteen minutes, I collected the sheets. My special education student had completed it along with everyone else. He received his sticker as always. I did nothing special or different that day.

The parent was dumbfounded. We met with the principal in the office afterwards and had a big laugh about how clever this special education student was—that he had conned his mother and entire support team into helping him get out of homework.

I worked with the student's mother to develop strategies that would help the child feel more successful at home. We started small—giving a handful of math problems at first. After a week, we added more problems that needed to be completed every day. Finally, we increased it to a sheet like everyone else had to complete. It worked. The student began looking forward to doing his work without prompting.

It really does take a whole team of educators to raise a special needs child. Each one builds a beneficial relationship with the student, like puzzle pieces that fit in to create a full picture of his or her personality.

Learning disabilities is a major challenge for researchers and educators. This chapter explores the limitations of "exclusionary" ways of classifying learning disabilities (definitions that classify learners based on the absence of certain traits or assets). It concludes with a discussion about more promising directions for classification research.

Conclusion

Meeting the needs of special education students requires additional attention, resources, and time on the part of teachers, educators, and administrators. Teachers need to institute strong routines to create the kind of structure these students need to thrive. Everyone involved in the student's life—including parents—must work as a team to ensure the child's success. The attention and care that these students require end up raising the standard of education for all students. Perhaps this is one more gift special ones give us.

Chapter 7

INTO THE FUTURE

"There is no greater disability in society, than the inability to see a person as more."
—Robert M. Hensel

"My needs aren't 'special'. How my needs are met may be different but they are the same needs as anyone else's."
—Autism Women's Network

*I*f you have read this far, perhaps you understand why I wanted to write this book—why I *needed* to write it. I wanted the world to know about Dorica—not just to tell a story, but to leave a legacy for her and every special child. I could sense Dorica's nonverbal messages compelling me to write. As you know by now, she is very persistent.

When I began the process, suddenly parents all around me began talking about the special nature of "disabled" children. I became aware of movies and documentaries on the subject, particularly about the obstacles and prejudices special children face and how they overcame them. I noticed a shift in how people were starting to view special children. It is like we are collectively waking up—gaining awareness that will enable us to create a new kind of future.

There have been many times in history when humans have made great leaps in understanding. Science gave us the knowledge that the Earth is round and propelled us to recognize our planet as just one in the vast cosmos. It compelled us to think differently about ourselves and contemplate the potential for life beyond Earth.

The human rights movements of the twentieth century, such as the civil rights, women's, and LGBTQ movements, expanded our notions of what it means to be human. They challenged our limited ideas about differences and invited us to consider the strength in diversity.

At a frustratingly slow pace, we are waking up to the havoc humans have wreaked on a finite planet. We are beginning to connect our personal and collective choices to the warming of the planet and the careless destruction of precious ecologies. Activists have prompted us to preserve endangered species and exercise greater compassion toward the other animals that inhabit this planet.

Likewise, a movement has been afoot to make the world more hospitable for special children. Not long ago, they were seen as less human and shamed into staying on the margins of society. As with other progressive movements, people, parents especially, started making waves. Schools listened and created special education curricula. The environment became more accessible for people with disabilities. The United States led the way to building access ramps to public buildings. We stopped institutionalizing special needs children and allowed them to be cared for in the community. This was revolutionary.

The movement on behalf of special needs children has had incredible success. But it is only the first step. While we have worked to make the world better for our special children, we still consider them disabled. We only recognize that they need us. We do not yet realize that we need *them*.

Special ones make this world a better place for all of us by freely sharing their love. They hold no prejudices, express no violence, and do not express the phobias and "isms" that plague human relations. They have no concern for money or the trappings of success. They are one-of-a-kind souls, pure and uncontaminated. They bring happiness to everyone around them. All humans respond to this kind of unconditional love. They show us the way back to a pure heart and soul.

We can let our special children lead us to create the kind of world we all yearn to live in. We can take the next step in this movement—toward greater societal consciousness of the special ones in our midst. It must begin with us as parents and advocates for our children. We must become fully aware of the special gifts of our own children.

Toward this end, I present fourteen questions that can help prompt introspection, a greater appreciation for your own special one, and perhaps launch a collective discussion:

1. What special events or insights surrounded the conception or birth of your special child?

2. Did you have dreams about your child before he or she was born? If so, what were they?

3. Did your child exhibit special traits or gifts from very early on? If so, what were they?

4. How did you deal with the realization that your child was and is handicapped? What was your child's diagnosis? What treatments were offered, and what prognosis did you receive for the future?

5. How did you grow into your role as a caretaker? What helped you cope?

6. What support system did you develop out of necessity (such as school, church, care settings, extended family)?

7. How did you adjust over the years to the demands of caring for a special one, which you knew could last a lifetime? Think about adjustments you made professionally, and regarding romantic relationships/marriage and friendships. What technologies did you employ? How did you set—or not set—boundaries?

8. Was your child a teacher, friend, or confidante to you? What were the special gifts s/he exhibited (such as gifts related nature, pets, spirituality)?

9. How did you integrate your special one into your neighborhood or community?

10. How did your child relate to siblings, friends, and extended family?

11. How did your child express his/her sexuality?

12. Is your child a "happy camper?" Why or why not? Where is your child now? (Home, board-and-care home, hospital?)

13. How do you see the future unfolding and what do you think you can do to help your special one?

14. Have you developed a plan for who will take care of your child when you cannot care for him/her anymore?

Take time answering these questions. They will help you create your own narrative about your experience with your special one. You may be surprised by the insights and awarenesses you gain.

A Note of Caution

Any discussion that we as parents have, and any activism that it leads to, will take place in a context in which science could develop the tools to alter our special ones' consciousness. Our current medical and social model sees our special ones as disabled, and gene therapies could be introduced to "cure" or "treat" these disabilities.

Any such medical interventions could bring benefit or harm, and perhaps both. I would be very reluctant to alter the specialness of Dorica. The more I read and hear about futuristic manipulations, the more careful and protective I become of Dorica. I believe we would need to have a serious discussion about this topic.

We might decide as parents to build a movement to say "no" to futuristic medical interventions. We as parents can and should decide what is best for our special ones. They are here for a reason, and we need to weigh the pros and cons before we interfere with their basic nature. Who benefits if we let science genetically engineer our children?

As I say this, I also feel compelled to consider the possibility that medical advances actually *could* bring benefit. For instance, a new discovery shows a connection between Down syndrome and Alzheimer's disease. Many people with Down syndrome develop Alzheimer's disease when they get older. Research shows that people with Down syndrome have an extra copy of chromosome 21, which carries the amyloid precursor protein (APP) gene. Too much APP leads to a build-up of protein clumps in the brain. By age forty almost all people with Down syndrome develop this condition and become at risk for Alzheimer's.

By understanding this mechanism, scientists could alter the immune system and develop a vaccine or cure for dementia and Alzheimer's. This could be available in five to ten years.[7] In this way, Down syndrome children could become our saviors in the future. So who am I to say that medical research could not bring good to mankind? My point is simply that any discussion we have as parents must be grounded in solid information and weigh the benefits and drawbacks of a given intervention.

Building a Global Heart

Humanity is slowly, collectively waking up. We are in a time of tremendous transition, an incredible opportunity to appreciate all of what we have on this beautiful planet.

With this book, I hope to add to this collective awakening by beginning a global conversation. As I explore in previous chapters, some cultures revere their special ones, while others see them as less human. What can we learn from each other? What wisdom can we share? How can we support each other and create a collective vision that includes our special children in the future of the human race? Could we build a Global Heart where our special ones show us the way?

Let us begin the second phase of this movement on behalf of special needs children. Let us work together, share ideas, strategies, and tips. And most of all, let us create a dialogue about the capacities of our special ones.

Technology provides us with incredible tools to communicate. I would like to extend a special invitation to parents to share their experiences. I have created a Facebook group (The Magic of Special Children) to get us started. Visit the page and request to join the group. Post your answers to the fourteen questions. Talk with me and the other parents and let's get a discussion going.

---

7 See LuMind Research Down Syndrome Foundation, www.lumindrds.org, and the National Institute on Aging, www.nia.nih.gov.

Further, let's call each other, meet each other, and create workshops. My contact information appears below. Feel free to reach out to me. Let's see what kind of world we can create together. I look forward to meeting you.

Astrid Cheney, Special Children's Specialist

Webpage: www.AstridCheney.com
Email: astrid.cheney@gmail.com
Facebook: AstridCheney
Facebook Group: The Magic of Special Children
Additional Support Facebook Group:
Special Needs Parents Support and Discussion Group

Appendix

TOOLS AND RESOURCES FOR PARENTS, CAREGIVERS, AND TEACHERS

The following are some resources I recommend, including books I found helpful in my search for information about caring for adult children with special needs:

How to Start a Home-Based Day-Care Business by Shari Steelsmith, 2011. As the title indicates, this book provides strategies for how to start a day care business. Even though it focuses on day care for children, the information easily applies to other setting such as board-and-care homes and adult care centers. I found the section on solving common problems to be particularly insightful.

Facing Learning Disabilities in the Adult Years: Understanding Dyslexia, ADHD, Assessment, Intervention, and Research by Joan Shapiro and Rebecca Rich, 1999. This book is written for learning disabled adults, high school and college students with learning disabilities, parents, professionals across disciplines, and the lay public. It translates theory into practical strategies through the use of case studies. It shows that individuals with learning disabilities can attain significant levels of success.

Sesame Workshop. In 2015, *Sesame Street* introduced Julia, a character with autism, along with an educational campaign, "See Amazing in All Children." The website contains information and resources for families, teachers, and caregivers. It includes guides to simplify everyday activities that can pose challenges for children with autism, including bedtime routines, going to the grocery store, and brushing their teeth. Visit https://autism.sesamestreet.org. There is also an app in the iTunes store.

The Special Needs Planning Guide: How to Prepare for Every Stage of Your Child's Life by John W. Nadworny. This book will guide you through the process to get your paperwork and plan in order.

Steps to Independence: Teaching Everyday Skills to Children with Special Needs by Bruce I. Baker. This book gives great advice for teaching life skills.

Yahoo's Parenting Website. Over the years I have found many good suggestions and discussions about caring for children with special needs on Yahoo's Parenting site: www.yahoo.com/parenting.

Listening to the Experts by Elizabeth B. Keefe, 2006. In this book, students with a wide range of disabilities talk about their past and present school experiences, special education-inclusive classrooms, practices, and policies. Teachers, parents, and educators share insights they gained from listening to the students.

Nolo's IEP Guide: Learning Disabilities by Lawrence M. Siegel, special education attorney and advocate, 2014. With downloadable legal forms from www.nolo.com, this book guides parents through the individual education plan process. It provides instructions, suggestions, resources, and forms to help parents understand the special education system and ensure their child's needs get met.

Young Children with Disabilities in Natural Environments: Methods and Procedures by Mary Jo Noonan, 2005. This book provides in-depth, practical information on assessing and intervening with children who have severe disabilities or autism spectrum disorders. It gives clear guidance about methods teachers can use in the classrooms. There is also a strong focus on cultural competence and practices concerning transitions from elementary to high school.

Working with Families of Young Children with Special Needs: What Works for Special-Needs Learners by R.A. McWilliam, 2010. This book—for teachers, educators, and families of young children—is often considered the training manual for service coordinators in early intervention programs. It provides research-based best practices for serving families of children with special needs from birth to age six.

In a Different Key: The Story of Autism by John Donvan and Caren Zucker, 2016. This book traces the history, science, and human drama of autism. It delves into the different expressions of autism, one of the most common syndromes in children today. This book provides valuable insights to help understand the spectrum.

Positive Strategies for Students with Behavior Problems by Daniel Crimmins, Ph.D. and others, 2007. Written for educators from grades K-12, this book provides guidance about how to effectively work with children with persistent or severe behavior problems. It introduces the systematic Positive Strategies method, which helps teachers understand why behaviors persist, as well as how to prevent problem behavior and replace challenging behaviors with better alternatives.

24th Annual Report to Congress on the Implementation of the Individuals with Disabilities Education Act by the United States Department of Education, 2002. The Individuals with Disabilities Education Act (IDEA), Section 618, is designed to assure the free appropriate public education of all children. This report, in four parts, provides comprehensive data and information about special education teacher quality, spending on special education, students served under IDEA, programs and services, graduation rates among students with disabilities, and much more.

Student Discipline: Individuals with Disabilities in Education Act, Report to the Committees on Appropriations. United States Senate and House of Representatives, United States General Accounting Office, Report No. GAO-01-210, 2001. One of the most insightful sections of this report is the discussion about how to create cooperative group structures—well-known techniques to facilitate engagement and cooperation among students of diverse backgrounds and styles—in the classroom.

Classification of Disabled Learners: Beyond Exclusionary Definitions by J.M. Fletcher, 1986. This chapter appears in pages 55-80 of Steven J. Ceci's *Handbook of Cognitive, Social, and Neuropsychological Aspects of Learning Disabilities*. Classifying learning disabilities is a major challenge for researchers and educators. This chapter explores the limitations of "exclusionary" ways of classifying learning disabilities (definitions that classify learners based on the absence of certain traits or assets). It concludes with a discussion about more promising directions for classification research.

Effective Schools: Teachers Make the Difference by D. Berliner, in *Instructor,* 99 (3), 1989, pp. 14-15. This article discusses using classroom rules as a way to support students in assuming responsibility for themselves and each other, and to create opportunities for students to become self-directed learners.

Elementary School Principals and Their Political Settings by William Bridgeland and Edward Duane, in *Urban Review,* 19(4), 1987, pp. 191-200. This article reports on a study of Detroit metropolitan area elementary school districts, which covers the relationship between school district income levels and characteristics of principals and school districts.

The Inclusive School: Sustaining Equity and Standards by Judy W. Kugelmass, 2004. This book addresses the needs of diverse populations and their interethnic interactions. Through the story of a progressively minded public elementary school, the author shows how committed educators can collaborate to maintain a creative, inclusive educational environment and still rise to the demands of stat-imposed standards.

Leading for Diversity: How School Leaders Promote Positive Interethnic Relations by Rosemary Henze and others, 2002. This book provides leadership models to help schools promote positive interethnic relations. Vignettes and case studies allow readers to assess and develop their leadership skills in interethnic relations by recognizing and developing their strengths, assessing how organizational structures support or constrain positive relations, understanding the nature of ethnic tension in the school, identifying the school's priority needs, developing a core vision of interethnic relations, creating and implementing a plan for promoting positive relations, and documenting the effectiveness of the plan.

Special Education's Changing Identity: Paradoxes and Dilemmas in Views of Culture and Space by A.J. Artiles, in *Harvard Educational Review*, 73, 2003, pp. 164-202. In this article, Artiles identifies "paradoxes and dilemmas" faced by special education researchers and practitioners who are seeking to create socially just education systems in a democratic society that is currently marked by an increasing complexity of difference.

Why Are So Many Minority Students in Special Education? Understanding Race and Disability in Schools by Beth Harry and Janette K. Klingner, 2006. This book discusses the complex constellation of culture, language, socioeconomics, family and community dynamics, and practices and processes within educational settings. It makes recommendations for improving educational practices and teacher trainings. It is a valuable guide for all educators within and outside of the special education system.

Dorica at Twenty-Five, 1994

Dorica at Fifty, 2019

ABOUT THE AUTHOR

    ASTRID CHENEY holds a master's degree in education from the University of California at Berkeley. She was an elementary school teacher for twenty-six years in Oakland, California, at one of the largest inner city schools, where she mentored many special needs children. The advice she offers in this book is therefore based not only on her success as a parent in raising Dorica, but also on her experience working with such children professionally.

    Ms. Cheney offers book readings through professional organizations she is part of, and holds workshops on the topics covered for parents and teachers. Her intention is to spark a wider opening of consciousness to what our special ones can offer, so that our children can benefit from better care and our world can benefit from their gifts.

www.AstridCheney.com

ABOUT THE ILLUSTRATOR

CHANTAL WOLF is a Canadian artist. Born in the United Kingdom, she grew up in the Toronto area, where her desire to make a difference led to a career in education supporting students with special needs. In this work, her passion for art so often served as a bridge of connection into their worlds. Wolf studied Illustration at Sheridan College, but is largely self-taught; over the years, she has continued to create art, completing numerous paintings, commissioned portraits and murals. In 2016, a diagnosis of Parkinson's Disease reignited her artistic passions and has fueled an exciting journey of creative exploration. She lives in Collingwood, Ontario.

www.ChantalWolf.com

PUBLISHER'S NOTE

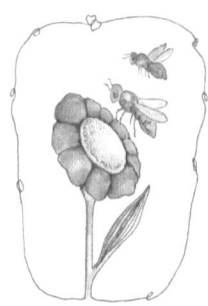

THANK YOU for reading *The Magic of Special Children: The Remarkable Story of Dorica With a Resource Guide for Parents and Teachers*. Please pass the torch of connection by helping other readers find this book. Here are suggestions for your consideration:

- Write a customer review wherever books are sold.
- Gift this book to friends, family, and colleagues.
- Share a photo of yourself with the book on social media and tag #astridcheney and #themagicofspecialchildren.
- Bring in Astrid Cheney as a speaker for your club or organization.
- Suggest *The Magic of Special Children* to your book club.
- Recommend *The Magic of Special Children* to the manager of your local bookstore.
- For bulk orders, contact the publisher at 828-585-7030 or email Orders@CitrinePublishing.com.
- Connect with the author at www.AstridCheney.com.

We appreciate your book reviews, letters, and shares.

www.ingramcontent.com/pod-product-compliance
Lightning Source LLC
Chambersburg PA
CBHW030154100526
44592CB00009B/264